Finding a Way Through
CANCER, DYING, *and* WIDOWHOOD

Also by Pamala D. Larsen

Lubkin, I., & Larsen, P.D. (Eds.)
Chronic Illness: Impact and Intervention,
2013, 2009, 2006, 2002, 1998

Jones and Bartlett

Finding a Way Through
CANCER, DYING, *and* WIDOWHOOD

A Memoir

PAMALA D. LARSEN

ARCHWAY PUBLISHING

Copyright © 2013 Pamala D. Larsen.

All rights reserved. No part of this book may be used or reproduced by any means, graphic, electronic, or mechanical, including photocopying, recording, taping or by any information storage retrieval system without the written permission of the publisher except in the case of brief quotations embodied in critical articles and reviews.

Archway Publishing books may be ordered through booksellers or by contacting:

Archway Publishing
1663 Liberty Drive
Bloomington, IN 47403
www.archwaypublishing.com
1-(888)-242-5904

Because of the dynamic nature of the Internet, any web addresses or links contained in this book may have changed since publication and may no longer be valid. The views expressed in this work are solely those of the author and do not necessarily reflect the views of the publisher, and the publisher hereby disclaims any responsibility for them.

Any people depicted in stock imagery provided by Thinkstock are models, and such images are being used for illustrative purposes only. Certain stock imagery © Thinkstock.

ISBN: 978-1-4808-0423-4 (sc)
ISBN: 978-1-4808-0425-8 (hc)
ISBN: 978-1-4808-0424-1 (e)

Library of Congress Control Number: 2013922829

Printed in the United States of America

Archway Publishing rev. date: 12/23/2013

In memory of Randy
1947–2012

Contents

Preface . . . . *xiii*
Introduction. . . . . *xv*
Prologue. . . . . *xvii*

Cancer

November 23, 2010 2
November 24, 2010. 3
December 3, 2010 5
December 6, 2010 6
December 16, 2010. 7
December 19, 2010. 8
December 20, 2010. 8
December 22, 2010. 9
December 27, 2010. 10
January 1, 2011. 11
January 3, 2011. 12
January 5, 2011. 12
January 6, 2011. 13

January 8, 2011	13
January 13, 2011	14
January 16, 2011	14
January 27, 2011	15
February 15, 2011	17
February 18, 2011	18
February 22, 2011	19
February 27, 2011	19
April 1, 2011	20
April 19, 2011	23
April 21, 2011	24
April 23, 2011	25
April 24, 2011	25
April 27, 2011	26
May 8, 2011	26
May 29, 2011	27
June 3, 2011	28
June 11, 2011	29
June 29, 2011	29
July 1, 2011	31
July 3, 2011	32
July 5, 2011	33
July 6, 2011	34
July 19, 2011	34
July 24, 2011	34
August 7, 2011	35
October 1, 2011	35
October 3, 2011	38
October 29, 2011	38
November 2, 2011	39
November 12, 2011	39
November 25, 2011	40

December 12, 2011. 40
December 31, 2011. 40
February 26, 2012 41
March 21, 2012. 42
March 25, 2012. 42
March 27, 2012 43

Dying

March 29, 2012. 46
April 7, 2012 46
April 8, 2012 48
April 15, 2012 48
April 20, 2012 49
April 22, 2012 50
April 23, 2012 51
April 25, 2012 51
April 29, 2012 52
May 2, 2012. 52
May 5, 2012. 53
May 10, 2012 54

Widowhood

May 16, 2012 58
May 20, 2012 60
May 29, 2012 61
June 4, 2012. 61
June 5, 2012. 62
June 9, 2012. 62
June 16, 2012 66
June 23, 2012 66
June 30, 2012 67
July 7, 2012 68

July 16, 2012	69
July 18, 2012	70
July 20, 2012	70
July 23, 2012	71
July 27, 2012	71
August 3, 2012	72
August 5, 2012	72
August 9, 2012	72
August 14, 2012	74
August 17, 2012	74
August 20, 2012	74
August 28, 2012	75
August 30, 2012	76
September 7, 2012	77
September 13, 2012	77
September 19, 2012	78
September 27, 2012	79
October 3, 2012	79
October 9, 2012	80
October 15, 2012	80
October 17, 2012	81
October 20, 2012	81
October 22, 2012	84
October 29, 2012	84
November 1, 2012	85
November 2, 2012	87
November 4, 2012	87
November 7, 2012	88
November 11, 2012	88
November 12, 2012	89
November 15, 2012	90
November 20, 2012	90

November 22, 2012	91
November 23, 2012	92
November 26, 2012	92
November 27, 2012	92
December 2, 2012	93
December 8, 2012	94
December 11, 2012	94
December 13, 2012	95
December 17, 2012	97
December 19, 2012	97
December 20, 2012	98
December 22, 2012	99
December 25, 2012	99
December 30, 2012	100
January 2, 2013	102
January 6, 2013	103
January 7, 2013	103
January 8, 2013	105
January 12, 2013	105
January 14, 2013	106
January 18, 2013	107
January 23, 2013	108
January 25, 2013	108
February 1, 2013	109
February 3, 2013	110
February 6, 2013	112
February 12, 2013	113
February 18, 2013	113
February 21, 2013	113
March 4, 2013	114
March 18, 2013	116
March 20, 2013	116

March 29, 2013 117
March 31, 2013 118
April 2, 2013 119
April 5, 2013 119
April 10, 2013 119
April 13, 2013 121
April 14, 2013 122
April 15, 2013 124
May 2, 2013 125
May 8, 2013 126
May 10, 2013 126

Epilogue *129*
Bibliography *133*

Preface

I'd never written in a diary or journal before, not even as an adolescent. However, when Randy was diagnosed with cancer, I felt drawn to put my thoughts on paper. My journal has been privy to my personal thoughts—often, thoughts that could not be spoken aloud. Thoughts that others might not understand.

I wrote the first entry in my journal the day Randy had a diagnostic test that revealed the cancer. Looking back, I have no idea why I even took a journal with me to the outpatient surgery center that day. I had work things to do, but I chose to take an empty journal instead. Throughout Randy's illness of eighteen months and my first year of widowhood, I wrote in my journal. It was my safe place.

While editing my journal for publication, I added some reflections, thoughts, and comments at various points. Sometimes now, from a distance, I can better understand what we were going through and what my thoughts were—but sometimes not.

This memoir is a conversation—first with myself and then, after his death, often a conversation with Randy. With loss, survivors have many questions, but they receive few answers. Each of us hopes that there is a magic answer, somewhere, to guide us through grief. But there isn't. We need to find our own way and our own answers. I'm still finding my way.

If you are now finding your way, may these words help you realize that you aren't going crazy, but are experiencing what others have felt and thought after a wrenching loss. My hope is that this memoir provides support or understanding in some manner. Many others have walked this difficult path. You are not alone.

Introduction

Cancer. It's esophageal cancer, stage IIIB. There's been no mistake. The pathology report has not been confused with someone else's. Randy has cancer. We sit quietly in the oncologist's office: Randy, our son Brett, and I. No one says a word. There are no words to speak, no questions that we need answered now. We are stunned. We had a normal life before … before cancer.

Prologue

The Larsens

When Randy and I received the diagnosis of cancer, we were living in Colorado. We planned to retire the following year or a year after that—he from his architectural firm and I from my position as professor/associate dean in a school of nursing. Along with my siblings, we were finishing the construction of a cabin in the mountains, which Randy had designed. It was a time full of promise.

Randy and I were married in 1969 after college graduation. After Randy's stint in the Army during the Vietnam War era, we established a new hometown in Colorado rather than return to Kansas, where we'd grown up. Randy, an architect, opened his first office in Colorado in 1977. I worked part-time as an RN at the local hospital and began teaching part-time. During those early years, our lives were blessed with three children: Brett, Amy, and Blake.

Randy's architectural practice flourished, and he began

specializing in university work, particularly designing research and development facilities. In the 1980s I returned to school for my master's and doctoral degrees, qualifying me to teach at a university. In the mid-1990s I wanted to try my hand at nursing education administration. Randy was supportive, so we packed up and moved—first to Kansas and then to North Carolina—to realize my dreams. In 2006 we returned to our Colorado hometown to be closer to our growing number of grandchildren. Randy opened a branch of the North Carolina architectural firm, and I became a professor and administrator in a school of nursing at a nearby university.

Each of our children married: Brett to Karrie, Amy to Shane, and Blake to Kareen. And from 2001 to 2012, the number of grandchildren grew to twelve.

Randy's family included his mother, Martha, and his two siblings, Jane and Roger. My family includes my father and four siblings: two sisters, Denise and Marisa, and two brothers, Craig and Doug. My siblings and I have always been close—so much so that in 2010, together, we built a vacation home in the mountains. Although it is truly a home, we call it "the cabin."

Randy and I were financially secure and tired of working, and we wanted to spend more time with each other. Then cancer became an unwanted guest.

Once, our family numbered twenty, and now we are nineteen.

Cancer

The disease that doesn't knock before it enters.
—Susan Sontag

November 23, 2010

The hustle and bustle of the surgery center. People everywhere: staff, family, and "with-'ems," as I call those who tag along or are the designated drivers for the trip home after a procedure—all in an accelerated world of activity. Where are they going? What are their stories? There are some tears, including my own, but most people are absorbed in their own worlds.

Randy has his intravenous (IV) line in place and has spoken with the anesthesiologist. There is talk of allergies. Somehow we had both forgotten his contact latex allergy from the early- to mid-1990s. Was he designing the Natural and Environmental Sciences Building project then? Was he forty-eight when he finished that project? Fifteen years ago? Where have the years gone?

I've tried in every way I can to calm myself this morning, but nothing's working. The uncertainty, the waiting, and just thinking how quickly this has all taken place won't allow it. It started with heartburn that seemed worse than normal and two incidents of food seeming to get stuck in his throat—once during the week of November 5 and again the following week. Randy's appetite had decreased in the previous few weeks, but nothing alarming, or so we thought. On November 16 we were off to our doctor's office, followed by an upper gastrointestinal (UGI) X-ray the following day, and back to our doctor's office the next day to receive the report. A large mass had been found in his middle chest area. A visit to a gastroenterologist on the nineteenth, and today an endoscopy. One week ago today, we were headed to our doctor for what seemed like a nasty case of heartburn. Surreal … all of it.

Is this how a diagnosis of cancer happens? A mass in the distal esophagus—is it three to four centimeters or four to five centimeters in size? I've forgotten already. The UGI report is blurry in my mind. I see it on my desk at home, but it seems distant, foreign, someone else's. Perhaps a mistake has been made, and it *is* someone else's report. Randy's results have been mixed up with those of someone who has cancer.

Randy is quiet as he waits to go from the prep area to the operating room area. We've talked about the possibilities, none of which are positive. Scar tissue? Not likely. Maybe a stage I or II cancer? Maybe it's nothing. Is this a dream? We've both read too much on the Internet. I need to hear a positive story, but I haven't found one yet. Last night I read that the Mayo Clinic does 150 esophagectomies a year.

The last few days have been tense. We're both walking on eggshells. We talk, and then we don't talk. It's difficult to find the right words. The uncertainty of it all is eating us up. How can you make a plan when you don't have all of the facts? We are both doers, but it's hard to "do" when you don't know *what* to do.

November 24, 2010

What will today bring? A computed tomography (CT) scan is scheduled for 9:00 a.m., and we hope that by this afternoon, the pathology report will be back from the biopsies that were taken during Randy's endoscopy. But this is the day before Thanksgiving, and I'm not optimistic we'll have the results. We already know that it is cancer; it was evident from the mass that was biopsied yesterday. The type of cell and the stage of the cancer, we do not know.

We had a family meeting with our kids (without the grandchildren) last evening, explaining what's going on. Up until then, no one had known anything. As expected, our kids' responses were mature, caring and responsible. How could we have raised such wonderful children? Surely there was some luck involved somewhere.

All of my siblings know about Randy's health, as do Randy's mom, his Aunt Helen, and Jane and Brad (Randy's sister and brother-in-law). Craig, one of my brothers, is going to tell my dad in person. With Dad's hearing loss, I can't imagine a phone call trying to explain it to him.

I'm in bargaining mode. What can I do so Randy will live? If I'm a better person, will that help? I know my prayers are begging, so I avoid praying at all. How stupid is that? But I'm afraid to ask for life because that seems selfish. How do I ask for my soul mate's life? Which always brings me back to why my faith seems so weak. Do I even have faith at all?

A few days ago I asked Randy if he believed in God, fully knowing how he would answer. He said no. He has called himself an agnostic for many years. Do I believe in God? I want to. I want to believe we have eternal life and that we will be with our loved ones again in some manner. But I struggle with this; I want it to be true, but it doesn't seem possible. Why can't I be a true believer? Not being a true believer is making all of this more difficult. I'm trying to have faith, but I feel like I'm failing.

December 3, 2010

Here we are, beginning the cancer journey. Not knowing where, when, or how it will go. We're scared, even at this first appointment with the oncologist. Will there be more tests today? Or will it be only a review of what we already know: that this is stage IIIB squamous cell carcinoma, two lymph nodes involved, no distant metastasis found. Staging for most types of cancer is stage 0 to IV, with stage IV indicating that the cancer has spread to other organs or sites outside of where it originated.

Brett, our oldest son, is coming to this appointment as well. Randy reminded me last night that he, Randy, had been with his own dad at the appointment when his father received his leukemia diagnosis. (Randy's mom had had jury duty that day and could not go to the appointment.) How many years ago was that? It was 1997, just a few months after my mother had died of ovarian cancer. Two parents dying of cancer in twenty months. My mother died at age seventy, and my father-in-law at seventy-three. And now my sixty-three-year-old husband has cancer? I want to wake up from this bad dream, but I don't think that's going to happen.

Dinner arrived this morning via overnight delivery from "The Charlotte Gang." The message said, "Thanks for all of the Christmas parties you had for us. Now it's our turn to feed you." There was a huge box containing ham, vegetables, and dessert. We have food for weeks, particularly since Randy is eating so little. We made some wonderful friends in the seven years we lived in Charlotte.

So here is the plan: an esophageal sonogram to complete the staging of the cancer, a positron emission tomography/computed tomography (PET/CT) scan, more blood tests, placement of a chemotherapy port, and a jejunostomy (for feeding) to begin the treatment. Chemotherapy and radiation will take place simultaneously, followed by an esophagectomy six to eight weeks later. Radiation will be five days per week for six weeks, and during that time Randy will have two cycles of chemotherapy, with fluorouracil (5-FU) and cisplatin. The National Cancer Institute and various oncology cooperative groups have performed seventy to eighty trials with this stage of cancer and type of cell, and these two drugs appear to show the most promise. We'll return in a week for a follow-up visit.

December 6, 2010

Everything that we talked about at the previous oncology appointment has been scheduled. We'll see the surgeon this morning to talk about the port and jejunostomy. Eventually, this surgeon will be the one performing the esophagectomy. Randy went early this morning for his blood work. He actually hasn't had any since before his hip replacement in October. Funny, six weeks ago he had a hip replacement, and now we hardly remember it. It's just a blip on the screen of life.

Over the past few days Randy's chest pain, coughing, and belching have become worse, mostly associated with eating. After two weeks he is already sick of soup, yogurt, and oatmeal. Mornings are best for him, as he feels better then. After lunch and a shower, the fatigue really hits him. Evenings are spent dozing on and off. It's just incredible that in two weeks he has come to feel as poorly as he does.

I just feel numb most of the time. It's still someone else's body and biopsy. I go from hopeful to pessimistic. I wonder, will this be our last Christmas together? We have had over forty-one years of married life, and I still want more.

December 16, 2010

At a doctor's appointment, again. This will be our new normal. Our lives are now dictated by tests and doctors' appointments. Today is the first visit with the radiation oncologist. From here we're off to do preadmission things at the hospital, to be ready for the insertion of his port and jejunostomy this weekend.

I don't think I reported on the PET/CT scan. The scan showed *no* metastatic lesions. Yay! However, this scan and the prior esophageal sonogram verified that there are two suspect lymph nodes. How our lives have changed—we now consider this good news.

The radiation oncologist seems more concerned than others about the lymph nodes. He also mentions a node in the supraclavicular area (above the collarbone) that will be treated as well. Randy's treatment will be very aggressive, because the radiation oncologist feels that the radiation therapy and chemotherapy together can eradicate the cancer. He doesn't say "cure." He also says that squamous cell carcinoma responds well to radiation, as compared with adenocarcinoma, an epithelial cancer that can also affect the esophagus. He is optimistic! Those are his words, not mine.

The treatments will begin the last week of December. The goal is to completely eradicate the tumor so when surgery occurs, the tumor will be essentially gone.

Going from one office to the next is tiring for both of us. I'm not sure what a normal day is anymore. We're both still working on our new normal. We don't know what it is, but we realize that we're not close to accepting it. I'm physically and emotionally exhausted. I take a sleeping aid at night, but always wake up fatigued and worrying about everything. At least my student grading is over for the semester, so there is a bit of a breather for me at work.

December 19, 2010

I wait as patiently as I can in the surgical waiting room. Because this is a Sunday, I'm alone in the room. We checked in at 7:30 a.m., and Randy was taken to the OR at 9:00. His chemo port will go into his left chest area. There is some question about what kind of tube will be used for the jejunostomy (J-tube) insertion because of his contact allergy to rubber. He had another EKG and answered questions that were similar to those he had already answered. Although the cancer journey began in November, this surgery and its results offer the first outward evidence that anything is wrong.

December 20, 2010

We're waiting to see the oncologist regarding the oxygen that accompanied Randy home after his chemo port and J-tube insertion yesterday. His oxygen saturation percentage (sats) continued to be in the low eighties after surgery—much lower than they should be—so oxygen became his new friend. A home oxygen unit was delivered. It sits in the hall, making constant noise as it cycles on and off. We've named it "The Big Lug." At least it has a fifty-foot leash, as Randy calls it, so he can go most anywhere on the first floor of our house. He tells me that he feels better today and that the every-four-hour pain medication is helping. His meals consist of soup and pudding.

Brett and Blake, our sons, went to the cabin today to meet with the builder. The cabin that my four siblings and I have built in the mountains is almost completed. Randy designed it and Blake did the structural engineering. We are eager for its completion.

December 22, 2010

Okay, the oxygen stays because his sats are still in the eighties. His sats need to be near ninety-five to get rid of the oxygen. So The Big Lug continues to sit in the hall.

Yesterday Randy started vomiting around five in the morning. I called the surgeon's office, and we headed to the hospital for an X-ray of the abdomen. Randy was exhausted by the end of the excursion, but the good news was that the X-ray was negative for any obstruction. Nausea and vomiting continued all day. He was either in bed or sitting in his chair in the living room with his eyes closed. His intake for the day was maybe three to four ounces of water.

Today is better. He is eating small amounts and his color is better. Today is chemo education day—and again trying to get rid of the oxygen. No luck, however. Whenever Randy starts to walk, his sats fall into the low eighties. Christmas is near and our family will be together, so The Big Lug sitting in the hall needs some explanation for the grandchildren. We have left it up to each set of parents to explain to their kids about Grandpa's illness. Our eleven grandchildren range in age from nine years to six months.

Chemo begins on January 3 and not on December 27, when the radiation therapy begins. Disappointment. All I can think is that radiation therapy is almost a week away, chemo is delayed, and the cancer continues to grow. There is a long list of prescriptions to prepare for his chemo, both pre-chemo drugs and post-chemo drugs. Pulmonary function tests have been ordered for next week to see what's going on with Randy's lungs—why he can't be weaned from the oxygen.

December 27, 2010

We had a wonderful Christmas Day, even though Randy couldn't eat anything. Then the vomiting started again yesterday evening, so we made an appointment this morning. The appointment ended with Randy being hospitalized to get his nausea and vomiting under control and to hydrate him. What a long process. We got to the hospital by 11:45 a.m., and even though he's a direct admission, it's 1:15 p.m. and he hasn't had any anti-nausea medication or IV fluids yet. It appears that many of his blood tests are abnormal.

January 1, 2011

It's the new year, and Randy is still in the hospital. You'd think that with all these days at the hospital, I would have written something—but somehow I didn't. My anxiety level was too high. Lots of ups and downs in the past week. Randy has been on total parenteral nutrition (TPN) for three days and is also being fed through his J-tube. TPN is given intravenously and is a unique liquid mixture of glucose, vitamins, minerals and other nutrients that specifically meet the patient's nutritional needs. Randy's J-tube feeding is a dense liquid of nutritional products that is given through a tube that is placed in his jejunum, a part of his small intestine. He's on an IV antibiotic now because one of his blood cultures came back positive for an infection. No eating—only ice chips.

Today Randy feels better and says this is the best he has felt since his J-tube was placed in December. Maybe home one of these days?

The days all run together now. I bring all my work to the hospital each day, but I can't focus on it. The easy things I can do, but the harder things—like preparing my materials to teach the nurse practitioner students about gerontological nursing—don't get done. I spend a lot of time keeping family informed about what's going on. It's tiring. There is always a voicemail or text to respond to.

We thought there would be bumps along the way, but didn't expect bumps before treatment even started. Randy has had two radiation treatments this week. Chemo should start on Monday.

January 3, 2011

Yay! Day one of chemo is finally here. He will have radiation today as well.

My days at the hospital have been exhausting. Thankfully it's only a twenty-minute drive from our house. I go home at night and am worn out. I keep hoping that I will sleep better at night, but it isn't happening. I left Randy's room early last evening, and it was nice to have some sort of evening at home. The dogs appreciated having company as well.

The TPN was discontinued yesterday, so maybe there is hope of going home. However, his only nutrition is his continuous J-tube feeding. They're still searching for this mysterious infection that showed up in a blood culture. He's doing pretty well today, even with chemo, and whenever possible is trying to run his office from the hospital.

January 5, 2011

Any illusion of going home before Friday or Saturday is gone. The doctors are tracking his diarrhea now, testing it for different bugs. I'm hoping it's the result of too much tube feeding. It's been running 120 milliliters per hour for fourteen hours today. Tonight it has decreased to 100 milliliters per hour.

I went to work today for a few hours. It was nice to have some normal activity in my day. Some friends and I went to lunch; it lasted for two hours as we tried to catch up on everything. One of these friends had a breast biopsy in December and has breast cancer. With Randy diagnosed on November 23, one of the school's secretaries on November 28, and now my friend, it's overwhelming to say the least. Cancer sucks!

How do these aberrant cells get started? This whole cancer journey is overwhelming. Some days I look at Randy and see tubes sticking out of him and think, *how can this be happening to us?* We're the lucky family. How can having cancer be lucky? Is it to make us appreciate life more? Have we been greedy and not thankful enough? Why? Why Randy? This should be me; cancer runs in the maternal side of my family. No cancer in Randy's family except for his father. A hip replacement and then, four weeks later, cancer. I just want this to go away. I want things to be normal again. But what is normal?

January 6, 2011

Looks like Randy will be coming home on Saturday. Lab values were good this morning, and he has felt better since his tube feeding has been decreased. I've had my training on his feeding pump. Now I need to figure out his medications. Randy and I talked today about how neither of us feels like this is real. I see the pumps and tubes and none of it seems real—or if it is real, it's not cancer.

January 8, 2011

Home! Tube feedings and IV antibiotics, but we're home. Lots of medications to crush for Randy's J-tube, but no oxygen this time.

January 13, 2011

A week since discharge—a week of appointments, IV antibiotics, tube feedings, and more. The radiation oncology office called last night to let us know that Randy's specialized radiation has finally been approved by the insurance company. This was the last appeal, an external one. If it hadn't gone through, then we were on our own to pay for it.

Randy weighed 175 on our scales at home today. He says that he was up to 215 during the last months before his illness. Somebody at his office asked about his hip. The hip replacement seems so long in the past and so insignificant, although it wasn't. But compared with cancer … No comparison. Again today, labs, radiation, but we're nearing the end of the IV antibiotics.

January 16, 2011

This absolutely takes the cake. We are in the emergency room because the dogs got tangled in Randy's feeding tube as he was feeding them this morning. The J-tube was out in a second. So here we sit, now into hour three, in the ER. After the dog event (at 5:30 a.m.) Randy started vomiting, so his surgeon has ordered a modified barium swallow to see if anything is passing through.

I am not a happy camper. This was so preventable. Isn't it common sense that you wouldn't be feeding the dogs with your pump going and dogs jumping everywhere? It just took one paw for everything to come out. Randy's surgeon says that if the tube had been in place longer—even just a few weeks longer—it could possibly be reinserted, but at four weeks it's too soon. Randy said that he wanted to help me out so I could sleep. But common sense says this is *not* the way to help out. Dogs are dogs.

January 27, 2011

I'm trying to find a new normal, but most of our days are unique. Randy's caloric intake and hydration, in general, are still not what they should be. He still has periods of vomiting. Some days he seems to have some energy: he did well at the cabin for a couple of days, and seemed to enjoy being around everyone. But then yesterday, at home, he slept the whole day. Karrie, one of our daughters-in-law, brought over their five children in the afternoon. It was great to see them. It seems that most of the time we are in "illness" mode; the grandkids made things more normal instead of the two of us bumbling around thinking about cancer.

I struggle to write in this journal, and I don't know why. Perhaps it's because nothing has really changed since Randy's diagnosis. He still has cancer, and it's not a curable cancer.

Reflections

Normal was both of us leaving for work each morning, attending grandkids' events, Randy cooking dinner, and the two of us sipping wine together on the deck in the evening. We were planning our retirement, road trips, days of not working. Then a new normal appeared, one of days with doctors' appointments, complications, outpatient procedures, Randy always feeling poorly, and living in the moment—not in the meditative Zen sense, because we chose to, but because we never knew what to expect next. Our days of the old normal disappeared.

February 15, 2011

Can something go right just once? Can Randy's potassium level be normal just once? Can he not have five straight days of IV fluids and electrolytes as an outpatient? Today he needed blood as well. He wanted to go by himself, so he left the house at 8:30 this morning; it's now 7:05 p.m. and he isn't home yet. How can being gone for more than ten hours be "good" for a patient with cancer? Then the surgeon's office called and said that Randy's chemo port can't be removed on the scheduled date because of something else. Oh yes, the port has to be removed because that's where the infection was. I'm mad, I'm tired. Can't something go right? How do people do this? Every day is different, so you can't plan on anything because it always changes. How do people work? How do they care for their families, with cancer always in the forefront?

Everyone asks, what can we do for you? I want to scream, "Take the cancer away. Let us have a normal life again." I can't stand this anymore. How does Randy handle this? He never says anything. Would I do that if I were he? He just sits, sleeps, and does crossword puzzles. We're just "here" and not much else. Each day is the same in some ways: read the paper, eat breakfast, and then head to a doctor or outpatient facility for something. Stay one hour? Maybe four or five hours? I told one of my sisters today in an e-mail that I could scream and cry at the same time. And that's pretty much what I want to do every day.

I so much want to go to the cabin next week, but it's not going to happen. Where is our time? Is this it? Work forever, get sick, and then die? Why can't I keep Sunday's sermon in mind? Lord, where are you in this storm? I need you, and I don't feel you anywhere. Give me a sign—anything. I need to know you are with me. I don't feel it. Is it because I don't know how to pray (which I don't)? Why don't I feel your presence? It's three months tomorrow since we first went to see our family physician about Randy's heartburn. I just can't fathom everything that has happened. I want this to be over.

February 18, 2011

Another day of waiting and sitting, something I don't do well. Patience has never been one of my virtues, nor Randy's either.

The infected chemo port is out. We got home yesterday around 2:30 p.m. and Randy slept until 6:00 p.m. I tried to wake him at 4:30, but he was too tired. He took some water and then vomited. He had some more water during the evening and that came up as well. Finally, at 7:30 p.m., he decided to go to bed and slept until seven this morning. He was still feeling lousy and went back to sleep in his chair.

Now we are at the oncologist's office. A number of lab results are abnormal, but not as bad as they've been in the past. Orthostatic hypotension with a blood pressure of 75/57 when standing. No wonder he feels so dizzy and weak. With no port now, it took four sticks to find a vein for his blood work. He's having IV fluids now, and then we'll see what his oncologist wants to do. Randy has been asleep the whole time since we've been here. What's next? Admitted to the hospital.

February 22, 2011

Home from the hospital last night. No vomiting since Friday evening. Randy seemed pretty good in the hospital after he received his IV fluids, electrolytes, and two units of blood. Yesterday he was very sleepy and couldn't wake up, but was ready to go home. Home by five and he slept in his chair until eight when I sent him to bed. He's still not up this morning at six thirty.

We see our family physician today. How could we *not* see a doctor each day? I'm reminded of a quotation from an article in the last edition of my nursing textbook: "I'm not a wife, but a caretaker."

We'll see how today goes. Randy has a proposal due for work this week. I'm not sure he is firing on all cylinders right now. I'm still hoping that we can go to the cabin later this week.

This is the hardest work I've ever done, hands down—and I can make him happy only twenty percent of the time. The rest of the time, something isn't right.

February 27, 2011

We have spent a wonderful four days and five nights at the cabin. Randy's potassium is still quite low, but he has been taking lots of oral supplements and has kept them down most of the time. He is feeling better and acting more normal. We've talked about the future and what it might bring as far as his health, but also retirement, resigning from his architectural firm. No matter the outcome, even if his health is okay post-surgery, days at his firm as a full-time partner are nearing the end.

The cabin has been so medicinal. The view from the cabin is as spectacular as we imagined it would be. Thursday night we went to our favorite restaurant up the road, so at least we were normal for a bit. Randy hasn't done any crossword puzzles, and I haven't read any books—surprising, but the time has gone by so quickly. Our builder came over yesterday and we went over some of the punch-list items.

I've taken several long walks that have been healing. I walked to the falls one day. It has been years since I've done that—but when you weigh a lot less and your back isn't on fire, you can do it. The falls is an awesome place to pray. I asked God to take Randy into his care, and acknowledged that it was his will as to what will happen. The burden is so heavy, and I fear it will become heavier. How many times have I said, *This doesn't seem real. How can he have cancer?* But now I see this frail, older-looking man who has lost forty to forty-five pounds, walking slowly, eating slowly, taking many medications, unable to exercise, and the list goes on. It is real.

We will be back at the cabin again in March, probably fairly close to when he'll have all of his scans again in preparation for his esophagectomy. I can't wait for this special time again.

April 1, 2011

No entries for March. The last few months are a blur. Doctors' appointments run into each other. Tests and test results run together. Bad days run together. But now the good days are returning. Randy has had three solid weeks of feeling good and lots of eating (at least a lot for him). He's gained six pounds in the last ten days, all the way up to 166. Today he went to his office in the morning, then to an appointment with the oncologist, and now to have another endoscopy. The PET scan results were great (amazing how your definition of "great" changes). The questionable lymph nodes had no metabolic activity. The esophageal tumor is greatly diminished, but still was "hot" because it has been only seven weeks since radiation ended. The esophagectomy has been scheduled for April 19. Next week he has a stress test since the PET scan showed coronary artery calcification in his heart.

But first, on the seventh we leave for the cabin—our respite for a week—and then back to fight the demon, cancer. I reread some of my first notes and saw much disbelief in what I'd written. I'm afraid it is still there. We celebrated forty-two years of marriage on March 29, and we both want more, though we are very aware of the odds. We are counting on two good years together and after that we feel that anything else will be a miracle. Will we get two years?

Reflections

During those first few months, there was much disbelief for both of us. It's hard to incorporate cancer, an unwanted visitor, into your life. But maybe denial and disbelief have a protective role to help you get through the tough spots. We tried to focus on the power of knowledge as some kind of control for us, even though our lives were spiraling out of control. Do we have all of the facts? Do we understand what was said at the last appointment? Should we seek a second opinion?

People ask you, what can I do for you? And you say nothing because all you want is to have the cancer go away. Everything else is insignificant.

From the first appointment with the oncologist I kept another journal to record Randy's doctor visits, his medications, weight, tube feedings, oral intake, everything "medical" until the day of his death. These medical journal entries were quite detailed. I believed if I had all the details on paper, then perhaps I could make sense of what was going on. Maybe I could problem-solve an issue. Maybe I could figure things out. Always maybes.

Randy's doctors believed that the tumor had been growing for at least a year. Were there signs along the way that both of us should have recognized? Randy had had heartburn ... since his twenties. What if he had been diagnosed six months earlier? Would that have made a difference? Would he be alive today?

April 19, 2011

The day of Randy's esophagectomy is here. The week at the cabin seems far away. We were at the hospital at 5:15 this morning for his surgery. Surgery didn't start until 7:30. It is now 10:00 a.m., and an operating-room nurse has given us an update. Randy is doing well. Surgery is still on the front side, to remove the esophagus. The thoracotomy, to put everything back together again, will come later. The nurse predicts that the surgery won't end until around 1:00 p.m. Our family is having quite a party here in the waiting room.

The cyst on Randy's face turned out to be a squamous cell carcinoma, site-specific but the margins aren't clear, so additional surgery will need to be done. Somehow I forgot to record this "little" problem previously. Probably three to four weeks before this current surgery, a boil-like bump appeared on his face. It was removed by our family physician in the office. It appeared to be a sebaceous cyst. However, pathology said differently, so it will need more care later.

An update at 12:15 p.m. and now another one at 2:30 p.m. Randy continues to do well. He hasn't needed any blood yet but probably will by the end of the procedure. His hematocrit was 32 this morning, and his potassium was 3.2. Geez, he just can't keep his potassium level normal.

Okay, changing of the guard for nurses. The report now is that the surgeon is working on connecting the remaining portion of the esophagus and the stomach. Randy's stomach is being pulled up to become a new esophagus, leaving a small pouch as his stomach. The nurse thought it would be at least another hour. A long, long day. Family and friends have come and gone all day, and I've received a number of texts and phone calls.

How will this end? I remember Randy's weakened state in January and February, and I can't imagine what the next few months will be like. My mind just becomes a blank as to the future. It's 3:40 p.m. now, the surgery is over, and Randy's mom and I are waiting for the surgeon to talk with us.

April 21, 2011

Two days post-op. Randy sat on the side of the bed yesterday and then today sat in a chair. He did well after getting all of his tubes arranged appropriately. The kids were here off and on all day. As a nurse, I feel compelled to write down every detail—as if somehow the details will bring clarity to the situation. Randy has an epidural in place from T-3 to T-10 for pain, an arterial line for blood pressure measurement, a bladder catheter with an internal temperature monitor, two chest tubes, heart monitor leads, a patient-controlled analgesia (PCA) pump, an anti-inflammatory drip for referred shoulder pain, a nasogastric tube, a couple of IVs running with an antifungal drug and an antibiotic, and his J-tube for feeding. I'm waiting to hear what his lab results are today. His hematocrit was 30 yesterday after two units of blood. His blood pH is slightly acidic. Otherwise, there is nothing remarkable. Except this whole journey.

Lots of texts and e-mails from family and friends. It's been hard to keep up with them. I've delegated some to my daughter Amy and my sister Marisa. I've not been on my work e-mail for almost a week. Even though I'm on sick leave, I feel guilty about my job. I haven't stayed all night at the hospital yet, even the first night, because I've felt everything was under control. I go home each evening around 9:00 p.m. and come back by 6:30 in the morning with the same feeling of exhaustion as when I left the previous night. Yesterday I went home for a two-hour nap during the afternoon and still couldn't keep my eyes open by evening.

April 23, 2011

The epidural for pain relief came out midmorning today. Randy is nervous about how his pain will be. He has walked in the room and been up in a chair and to the commode as well. He's doing well, I think. He has a barium swallow scheduled for Monday to see if the connection between his esophagus and stomach is patent. Same number of tubes, no change in that. It's snowing today, on April 23. Nothing is sticking, but the snow has been coming down softly and gently since 6:00 a.m.

April 24, 2011

Today is Easter. Randy had a rough night. Up to the commode several times with diarrhea. With the epidural gone, he is in much more pain. His blood pressure started increasing during the night as well, so a new IV drip was ordered to lower his blood pressure. The drip produces a side effect of a headache, so he isn't feeling well. His catheter is bothering him this morning, as well as some numbness in his neck. Just a crummy day for him.

April 27, 2011

Randy's chest tubes and catheter are out—as well as his PCA for pain, so it's back to oral pills for pain. He was transferred from the step-down cardiovascular unit to the surgical floor this afternoon. Randy had a swallowing evaluation yesterday (in addition to his barium swallow) that showed he was aspirating slightly, so his diet was changed to a full-liquid/thickened-liquid diet. Not exactly tasty, but he's eating it. Then a cardiovascular surgeon taking call for Randy's surgeon ordered a soft diet. I told the nurses his diet wasn't right, that his surgeon had said he would be on liquids for close to a month. The dietitian came up as well, and I explained it again. But no one listened to either Randy or me. So much for what the patient has to say in the matter. So he had a little roast beef last night. Randy's surgeon made rounds late in the evening and asked Randy what he had had for dinner. He told him roast beef, which obviously wasn't the right answer. So it's back to liquids again as it should be.

May 8, 2011

It's Mother's Day. Where does the time go? Randy came home from the hospital on April 30. It has been an uneventful time so far, for which we are thankful. He had an appointment with the plastic surgeon this past week to follow up on the minor surgery on the squamous cell carcinoma on his face during his hospital stay. All margins are clear. After a visit to the surgeon's office this past week, staples from both incisions are out. Randy continues his

J-tube feeding for twelve hours at night. He's taking around five hundred milliliters orally a day; in other words, two cups a day. He is better than a week ago, but I keep hoping for more progress, particularly in the eating department. I had hoped that we could decrease his tube feedings by now.

In the meantime, I had a trip to central Nebraska for the funeral of one of Randy's aunts. I took Randy's mother and another aunt with me. While I was gone, our son Brett stayed one night and our daughter Amy the other night. Someone else was with Randy during the day.

Some more tests and a barium swallow this week plus some lab work. We're hoping that his diet can be increased if everything is okay. If only his appetite would improve.

May 29, 2011

Randy has been on a plateau of sorts for maybe the last two weeks. He's taking lots of naps, and his eating has decreased so much that I increased his tube feeling last night. We're both discouraged. His weight was 152 yesterday, dressed with shoes. He told me yesterday that he is nauseated a lot of the time, but he hadn't told his surgeon's nurse when she did her weekly telephone check-in with him. He looks like a frail old man and definitely looks ten years older than when we began this cancer journey.

We are headed to the cabin tomorrow but wondering how that will go. Will the altitude (eight thousand feet) bother him? Will he be able to take a short walk or two? I'm scared. He just seems to be disappearing before my eyes. We don't talk much. He often just sits in his chair with his eyes closed. Yesterday, I had had enough. I decided to take over the structuring of his food and exercise. He doesn't have any appetite, so he doesn't eat, but I'm trying to get him to take two or three bites every hour or two. I'm going to divide up his exercise into small blocks of time, maybe three to five minutes, during the day. Will any of this make any difference? I don't know. In the back of my mind I'm always wondering, is the cancer still there, waiting for the right time to rear its ugly head again?

June 3, 2011

Another beautiful day at the cabin. Lots of sunshine, temperatures in the 70s with an occasional breeze. I've done nothing while we've been here, just read and walked.

Do I think Randy is better? Strange, the different definitions of "better" that I think of now. Some days, yes, and some days, no. He still eats so little, even on his good days. We've switched back and forth between 480 and 720 milliliters of tube feeding each night, depending on his eating. He continues to have reflux and nausea that is hard to predict. Some days it occurs between 3:00 p.m. and 6:00 p.m., although yesterday it started at noon. He gags, is nauseated, and feels lousy for a while. What should we expect? We don't know anymore. The altitude has affected his breathing somewhat. We're home again on Monday, and it's back to work for me. Appointments with the surgeon and oncologist next week to try to figure out where we go from here.

June 11, 2011

Finally Randy has had some relief from the nausea. He seems like a new person and all the nausea is gone because of a change in his pain medication. Gone is the hydrocodone and back again are the fentanyl patches. I see the old Randy now. He is eating as well as he can and gained a couple of pounds this past week. He didn't even take a nap yesterday, which is amazing, and even went with me to pick out mulch for the planting beds. Randy's oncologist says that the chance of recurrence is thirty to forty percent. The first two and a half years are of the most concern. He will have scans every three months during that time. The first one is July 8. I'm excited that he is feeling good again!

June 29, 2011

I don't even know where to begin. I look at my last entry and can't believe all that has transpired.

I got home from seeing my dad in Kansas Thursday evening, June 23. My dad has bladder cancer, and I went with him to an oncology appointment. Randy was doing well when I left. When I arrived home that evening, Randy showed me a rash on his abdomen. It didn't mean much to me. He wasn't on any new medication that might be the cause.

On Friday the rash was a little worse, and he also began complaining of a side ache. I was sleeping upstairs again because of the noisy feeding pump. We always keep our cell phones by our beds in case he needs something in the night. At 4:45 a.m. on

Saturday morning he called, saying that he had intense pain and nausea. He had turned his feeding pump off around 4:00 a.m. to see if that would make a difference, but the pain hadn't changed. I called our surgeon's on-call number and a call back said, "Go to the emergency room." A CT scan of Randy's abdomen indicated he had a kink in his small intestine, and so began another hospital stay. His admitting doctor was not his surgeon, but another doctor on call. That doctor didn't feel comfortable with how Randy was doing, and ordered a consult from a general surgeon. So we waited to see if bed rest, having nothing by mouth, and IV fluids would help the kink work its way out.

The surgeon came in late Saturday morning and said that the last X-ray showed a partial obstruction. He said, "Let's do a small bowel follow-through," meaning that Randy was to have four hundred milliliters of contrast through his J-tube and they'd see what would happen.

Randy returned to the floor around 11:30 a.m. in a miserable state. He was in terrible, terrible pain that pain medication did not touch. The vomiting began around noon and continued until 2:00 p.m., when the surgeon said we'd need to take care of the obstruction surgically. Randy went into surgery just before 3:00 p.m. and was out around 6:00, going straight to the Surgical Intensive Care Unit (SICU) on a ventilator. He was unable to breathe on his own. His vital signs were unstable.

I saw him briefly. He was heavily sedated and was not aware of my visit. I left his room so that the physicians and nurses could continue to work with him—his tubes, his drips, his pumps. I was in one of the family lounges with my sister Marisa and her husband, daughter Amy, daughter-in-law Kareen, with sons Brett and Blake on the way, when a Code Blue was called for room

2110 in SICU. I screamed. That was Randy's room! He had no pulse or blood pressure. With treatment, he responded within a minute. Everything after that is a blur. Many drips were running, the ventilator pressure required continuous adjustment, blood was being constantly drawn for tests. After hearing the code called, I remember trying to walk to SICU with Marisa and Amy holding me up because my knees were buckling. The tears flowed. The unexpected—or maybe it is to be expected with cancer—had happened again.

The hospital chaplain met with all of our family around midnight. The news from SICU continued to be "instability" and "critical condition." Amy and I stayed the night in one of the family lounges. I got up every couple of hours to see him, but the news was never good. A nightmare. We were living a nightmare.

July 1, 2011

Nightmare day number what? Randy's ventilator settings continue to be tweaked. His sedation has been lightened significantly, but he isn't responding. His surgeon is planning on doing a tracheostomy either tomorrow or the next day. Some bloody stool was taken to the lab and diagnosed with the *Clostridium difficile* (C.diff.) bacterium, so he has isolation precautions. I forgot to mention that he has shingles as well, thus explaining the rash on his abdomen. Somehow I never put the pieces of the puzzle together. Shingles seem so minor compared to what he is experiencing now.

Randy is extremely restless in bed and picking at things. He is now physically restrained to prevent him from removing his ventilator and numerous tubes. The plan is less sedation (hence the need for restraints) since he continues not to wake up on his own. The J-tube feedings continue and now total parenteral nutrition (TPN) is running in his central line. When I put everything down on paper, it seems never-ending.

Oh, I forgot to add a new diagnosis to the list: Acute Respiratory Distress Syndrome (ARDS). When I remember patients with ARDS from my nursing practice, such patients are severely compromised, unresponsive, and have a low chance of survival. It's clear that none of this is ending soon. I'm worried about quality of life versus quantity of life. I'm overwhelmed and confused. I've slept the past six nights in the family lounge with one of my family members. I'm exhausted, but this is about Randy, not me. We had hoped for two years together, but it's only been eight months since his diagnosis. Where is this going?

July 3, 2011

It's Sunday. Randy's ventilator settings are still too high, and he continues to be unresponsive, even though he has little sedation. Things aren't going anywhere. I'm headed to the family lounge, my home away from home, to take a nap. My prior seven or eight nights (I'm not sure how many nights I've slept at the hospital) have been exhausting—an hour of sleep, then up to check on him, then two more hours and up again to see how he's doing. I have prayed so many times during this hospitalization, but today I just couldn't get the words out to ask for his recovery again. So instead I said,

God, I'm finished praying to you about Randy. I'm tired of doing it, so I'm quitting now and turning it all over to you. I give up.

I woke up around 1:00 p.m., and Randy was better. His ventilator settings had been turned down and he was beginning to respond, and discussion about the tracheostomy on July 4 or 5 went away. Randy wanted to talk but couldn't because of the ventilator, so paper and pen it was. Although his writing was difficult to read, I could see that he was asking about our kids. It was Fourth of July weekend, so I explained that Blake and Amy and their families had gone out of town, reluctantly, but Brett and his family were in town. I asked if he wanted Brett here and he emphatically nodded yes. He continued to write notes to Brett and me the rest of the day. Thank you, Lord!

July 5, 2011

Randy's still doing well after being extubated for twenty-four hours. Oxygen is at five liters per minute and his saturation rates continue to be in the low nineties. So far, so good. He starts liquids this morning. His arterial line and the surgical drain in his abdomen are gone. He is actually sitting in a chair reading the paper this morning.

I'm overwhelmed with the last nine-plus days. I wonder how many more times events like this will occur. This is his fourth hospitalization in 2011, and it's only July. Is he cancer-free? His next scan was scheduled for July 8, but with his surgery and hospitalization, that scan has been postponed until August.

July 6, 2011

Randy is eating scrambled eggs this morning. His tube feeding has been discontinued to see if he can get his appetite back. Catheter is gone as well. He is being transferred to the surgical floor today!

July 19, 2011

The days run together. Randy was discharged from the hospital on the tenth, just fifteen days after going to the emergency room. My emotions have run the gamut over these last days since he's been home. Some days I think he's better and other days not. We are on a permanent roller coaster. Change: that's the one thing we can count on.

July 24, 2011

A great day yesterday celebrating Randy's sixty-fourth birthday, Lainey's first birthday (grandchild #11), Abby's eighth birthday (grandchild #3), Amy's thirty-seventh, and Blake's thirty-fourth. I can think of so many times since November that I thought Randy wouldn't see his birthday. Finally, new medication is helping his nausea and increasing his appetite. He's eating again and his mood is improving. He's eating frequently and in small amounts, but that's the way it will be for the rest of his life with his new esophagus. I'm hoping that when he weighs himself this week, we'll see a change for the better. Maybe things are starting to look up?

August 7, 2011

Another few days when Randy doesn't feel well. It's nausea again. Unfortunately we are at the cabin, which makes it harder to tolerate not feeling well. It seems like he never feels well at the cabin.

We had thought that the new drug was working; it seemed to be, for ten days or so. But now everything is back. This just never ends. We're coming up on nine months since that first appointment with our family physician when this all began. The good days seem few and far between. I feel like crying all of the time. This isn't a life; it's just going through the motions. Is this the way it will be until he dies? I'm tired of being a caregiver. I don't have much of a husband anymore. He doesn't talk much. The television is his companion most of the time. I wonder, is it the cancer? Is nausea always going to be his life from now on? He isn't gaining any weight.

I'm sitting on a park bench by the lake in the small village where our cabin is located. Families all around, laughing, talking, playing. It makes me lonely, but I'm just as lonely at the cabin since Randy is feeling poorly. Another vacation. Well, not really. Such a wonderful cabin—and we can't enjoy it.

October 1, 2011

September finally turned around for Randy, and particularly the last two weeks have been great. The J-tube is out and all remnants of its existence are gone from the house. He is eating well and maintaining a weight of 150 to 152. His spirits have improved immensely since the tube has been out. He says that this is the best he's felt since mid-June before his emergency surgery. He's acting the most normal I've seen him since he was diagnosed.

Randy loves his cars. A couple of weeks ago, when the time was nearing for his next PET scan, he talked about trading in his sensible car, a hybrid Camry, for a new BMW. He was trying to decide whether he should do it if the results of the PET scan were good—or if the results were bad, was that a better reason? I laughed at him and said, really, does it make any difference? He sheepishly said, well, no, it doesn't. The next day he called me at work and said to stop by the dealership because he wanted me to test-drive some cars, something he had been doing most of the day. By late afternoon he was driving away in his new BMW. He loved that car like no other car he'd ever had. Was it because he knew it was the last car he would ever drive? When his PET scan results came back "cancer" the next week, he was so glad he'd made the purchase. The grandkids named it "the race car" and Randy and I called it that as well.

We're at the cabin. It's a perfect weekend weatherwise, and Randy feels great. We can't ask for anything more than that. We're driving up Pikes Peak this morning to see the fall leaves. In the race car, of course.

Reflections

Two major surgeries within a nine-week period. Overwhelming for both of us. The June surgery and complications made the esophagectomy seem like a walk in the park. Randy remembered being dropped off at the curb of the emergency room in June while I went to find a parking place, but remembers nothing of those nightmare days except the last couple of days on the surgical floor. I'm thankful he remembers little.

After those couple of months, we began to be afraid to make plans. We often felt like we were prisoners in our own house, even though we had always been homebodies. We were hesitant to go anywhere. We were going through the motions of life, trying to be optimistic, but waiting for the other shoe to drop.

Like other nurses, I often thought I knew what a family was going through with cancer or other chronic illnesses. I thought I knew, but I didn't. Susan Sontag talks about "that other place." She writes, "Illness is the night-side of life ... Everyone who is born holds dual citizenship, in the kingdom of the well and in the kingdom of the sick ... Sooner or later each of us is obliged, at least for a spell, to identify ourselves as citizens of that other place."

We advocate that an illness shouldn't take over an individual's life, that the individual is more than the illness. But in reality, one's life is often one's illness. Life revolves around doctor appointments, tests, how many times you've vomited today, fatigue, IV antibiotics for an infection somewhere, and so it goes. Hospitalizations become a blur as to what happened when. That other place. I didn't know until now.

October 3, 2011

The worry hanging over our heads now is the recent CT scan that showed two small growing spots on Randy's left lung. These spots were also on his August CT scan, but were smaller and considered insignificant. The thinking at the time was that the spots were remnants of his ARDS from June and July. Now, one spot has doubled in size (to the size of a dime) compared with the previous scan. Last week Randy had a PET scan and also an echocardiogram of his heart because fluid has been accumulating around his heart. Our next oncology appointment is Thursday. How can he feel so well and have a spot on his lung? The continuing saga of cancer.

October 29, 2011

The forty-sixth anniversary of our first date; 1965 seems so far, far away. Randy continues to feel great. He is trying to go out with his golfing buddies and play a bit each week, but a storm came through this week so no golf.

The lung spot that we've worried about since August is real. It's cancer. So now we're off to chemo land again. Chemo every week for three weeks, then one week off, and back at it again. He is taking two chemotherapy drugs as well as a monoclonal antibody. Somehow we will get through this, but I don't know how.

November 2, 2011

I'm sitting in the outpatient surgery center lounge just like I did on the day of his first endoscopy in November 2010. Today Randy is having a dilation of his esophagus. Thank goodness he could get this done before chemo starts tomorrow. Because his esophagus is mostly his stomach, dilation is part of his treatment regimen every five to six months. With chemo coming up, we didn't want to take a chance that his esophagus would become constricted during chemo when he needs good nutrition. So here we go again.

November 12, 2011

We're at the cabin for a short weekend. Two weeks of chemo down and more to come. Randy has done fairly well with the chemo. Nausea off and on, although medication has helped. He does have a rash on his head, neck, and back due to the monoclonal antibody. I thought he was eating okay, but he lost four pounds in a week. He is supposed to do three or four cycles of chemo to see if the spots on his lung shrink or if others pop up. So life continues to be in limbo. Always what-ifs.

Somewhere in the last six to eight weeks, I've lost my way. Depression and tears seem to always be present, and that started before we knew about the cancer in his lung. Anyway, I'm adding an antidepressant to my medications. Better living through chemistry.

November 25, 2011

A great Thanksgiving yesterday with all children and grandchildren present, along with Karrie's parents and sister. Another chemo day today. This is the long day, with all three drugs and lots of IV fluids. We should be out of here by 6:00 p.m., after having arrived at 8:00 this morning.

December 12, 2011

Time for another esophageal dilation. The first one helped a great deal, so here's hoping that this one will as well. Two full cycles of chemo completed with a CT scan this afternoon. We have an appointment with Randy's oncologist on Wednesday. Has this chemo made a difference? Randy is tired all the time and naps frequently. The nausea comes and goes.

How many times have I been in this waiting room in the last twelve months? We wanted a couple of years together, but the quality times in this first year are few and far between. We remember the first couple of weeks of April, three weeks in June, and then September and October, but that's about it. Time keeps going faster and faster. We both want to slow it down because we don't know how much more time we have.

December 31, 2011

Good riddance to 2011, and here's hoping that 2012 will be better.

But how real is that possibility? You know in your heart that the chances of it being better are slim to none.

We've had a wonderful week at the cabin between Christmas and New Year's. We've done puzzles, played Scrabble, read, watched football, and it's all been heavenly. The effects from chemo are finally receding. The CT scan before Christmas showed mixed results (one lung tumor shrank somewhat, one stayed the same, but a new one was found). Options are few. This time it will be CyberKnife for the lung tumors. CyberKnife treats discrete tumors, in the lung and other organs, with beams of high dose radiation in hopes that the radiation will destroy the tumor. Randy will have four treatments in January. The radiation oncologist is confident that this will eradicate the tumors. But then, we've heard this before. We are encouraged, but always wondering when the next tumor will pop up. Ten to twelve weeks post-CyberKnife, Randy will have another scan.

February 26, 2012

Almost two months since I've written. CyberKnife was over on January 26. Thankfully, there were no side effects. Now we wait until the PET scan in mid-April. Will the lung tumors be gone? Will other spots show up? Randy has been feeling good, eating and working some. He is headed for Charlotte, North Carolina, tomorrow, his first flight since August 2010. Charlotte is where his firm's main office is located. He'll be back on Thursday, and then off to Phoenix with his golfing buddies. Amazing that he feels this strong. Is this his last burst of energy? I haven't spent a night away from him for over a year. Things will go well, I'm sure, but I'm anxious.

March 21, 2012

It's the first day of spring. Will we have another one together? We just returned from a road trip to San Diego and Phoenix, and Randy was admitted to the hospital upon our return. He had developed intense abdominal and chest pain while we were in San Diego. Only ten days ago, Randy played eighteen holes of golf at the Torrey Pines North Course. He was on cloud nine—but that night the pain became intense. We headed east toward home, but stopped a night in Phoenix to see friends. Unfortunately, Randy ended up in the emergency room there. Nothing acute was found on a CT scan, and stronger pain medication was prescribed. We returned home as quickly as we could.

Yesterday Randy had a thoracentesis to remove fluid from between the outside of the lungs and the chest wall. They removed 650 milliliters of what we called "brown ale." No pathology report yet. Pain management has not gone well. I have no words.

March 25, 2012

The day we knew would come someday came yesterday. The pain in Randy's chest is more cancer in his lung. There are only two options: a clinical trial or hospice. It was Randy's decision that he not be in a clinical trial, saying that he knew the results would help someone else, but that he was tired and didn't want to do this anymore. A clinical trial could be located anywhere (there aren't any in our state now for his cell type). And it might not give him any more time. We need to get the pain under control now. We sat on the patio outside of the hospital cafeteria twice yesterday. Few words passed between us.

March 27, 2012

Randy got a referral to hospice yesterday, and the admission nurse has come for her intake assessment. My question to hospice was about esophageal dilation: would it be allowed? Thankfully, yes, it is okay, because eating is comfort care.

The tears come often now. My sister Denise, from Kansas, was here for a day. It was wonderful to see her. And it will be good to have Randy home. The weather lately has been beautiful. He can soak up the sun on the deck.

There is a chance that a palliative radiation treatment might lessen the pain, at least temporarily. It's scheduled for tomorrow night, and then we'll go home on Thursday, March 29—our forty-third wedding anniversary. We are hoping for some good months before things go downhill. Best guess from the oncologist is three to six months. I still can't believe this is happening. This is someone else's life. Hospice? I am numb.

Reflections

We had such high hopes for chemo and CyberKnife. I think back to the summer of 2011 when things were bad. Somehow you think you have conquered the worst. But now this. As I look back now, I realize that Randy was never cancer-free, never in remission. I probably knew this intellectually, but it was something I never thought about or talked about. I hid it in some part of my being. The cancer was always there. Aberrant cells, sitting in wait, waiting for their time. What is the trigger for these cells? I've always believed that everyone has such cells, sitting, waiting. For some individuals there may be an environmental trigger. For others perhaps it is a genetic trigger. Something causes these cells to become malignant. The mystery of cells. I don't understand.

Dying

You imagine that you'll grow old together.
You want a fairytale ending to your love story.
But some love stories don't end that way.

March 29, 2012

Today is our forty-third wedding anniversary, and Randy is home from the hospital. Hospice was here by 10:30 this morning. More pain medications, more naps, a conference call with his partners in there somewhere, and then back to sleep. His pain is still not under control. Perhaps there will be answers tomorrow. There is no anniversary celebration today.

April 7, 2012

The days blur. The first two days Randy was home, he slept most of the time. I blamed it on his pain medication. There have been some changes in his medication now, and he is awake more often. He is still dreadfully weak and fatigued. He has oxygen on all of the time now, so The Big Lug is in the hall again, complete with the fifty-foot leash. Amazingly enough, Randy played seven holes of golf yesterday with this golfing buddies, oxygen in tow. It was hard, as he has no strength to hit the ball, and he rarely finished a hole, but he was outside with his friends—all of whom he has known for over thirty years.

Neither of us can understand why he's going downhill so quickly. The first weekend of March, in Arizona, Randy and his golfing buddies played seventy holes of golf in two and a half days. A couple of days after that, we headed out on our road trip. He played the North Course at Torrey Pines on March 12. The pain started that night, and although we'd known the cancer would come back, we didn't expect such a downhill course. In the hospital, one day Randy's oncologist told him he had perhaps two months to live, and another day told him three to six months. We chose to believe the three to six months. But it doesn't make any difference now. I don't think he will live to see June.

When Randy left the hospital he weighed around 130 pounds, but he is less than that now. No appetite whatsoever. Last night he was talking about the fall 2012 elections and said, "It's hard to believe that I won't know the outcome." I see his decline, but it doesn't seem real. Sometimes I wish we had had an anniversary picture taken in March—but it would be so painful to look back and see this person, my husband, not looking like himself. This thin, gaunt person is not the man I've been married to for forty-three years.

His morphine is every four hours around the clock now. We go to bed early most nights, and I set an alarm and get up and give it to him so he doesn't miss a dose.

In February, while watching the Pebble Beach Pro-Am golf tournament, Randy had decided that he wanted to go to Pebble Beach with our sons and be there on his sixty-fifth birthday in July. Reservations were made, and he was excited to look ahead to something special. Today the Pebble Beach trip seems impossible. Maybe we can get to the cabin again instead. Even with his oxygen, I worry that the cabin's altitude is too high and he'll be miserable—but at least if the cabin doesn't work out, we could leave quickly and come home.

Randy told me last night that his bucket list doesn't matter, that he just wants to spend time with me at the cabin. He mentioned Pebble Beach, but said our road trip in early March was more important.

We have received lots of emails from folks, including a number from high school classmates, wishing him well, even though it's been forty-five years since he graduated from high school.

Tomorrow is Easter.

April 8, 2012

Easter Sunday and all kids and grandkids were here today. We had our annual Easter-egg hunt. This year we divided it into the big kids' hunt and the little kids' hunt. Kareen took a picture of Randy and me on our deck.

April 15, 2012

The Pebble Beach trip has been cancelled, and the substitute trip of playing golf with the boys at the Broadmoor is off as well. We were going to have our sons meet us at the cabin, and then they would go to the Broadmoor for golf. Physically, Randy didn't think he could ride along in the cart, let alone play golf. Maybe we can still go to the cabin this weekend.

Each day he is weaker. He has adrenalin for certain work-related things, but that is it. It has been nice to have Jane, Randy's sister, here for a few days. We've sat around and talked, not doing much of anything. Randy told me tonight that he's having trouble swallowing. Is it the cancer or just the normal stricture he feels before having his esophagus dilated?

April 20, 2012

No cabin for this weekend. Randy decided that he couldn't go. In some ways, that is for the best. At least I won't remember our last time at the cabin as a bad experience. We had several of those bad experiences at the cabin last year. That's enough. I'd like to remember our time in February of this year and the last week of 2011.

Today Randy was up for a couple of hours and then back to sleep for five hours. He had maybe a quarter-cup of a smoothie all day, and it's now 4:30 p.m. Maybe not eating speeds up the growth of the cancer—and is that a bad thing at this point? I see this shell of a man, between 120 and 125 pounds, who doesn't talk much, eats nothing, and sleeps a lot. This isn't Randy.

Our cemetery plots are purchased. I had visited the cemetery a couple of weeks ago by myself, but I needed to make a final decision, and Randy wanted to go with me this time. I hate the names that cemeteries give certain areas. The Garden of Tranquility. We both have little twenty-by-twenty-inch plots for our ashes. Next week I'll tackle the memorial service.

With esophageal cancer you know that death is a common outcome, but somehow you think you'll be different. You'll win the fight against cancer; you will be the miracle. But it turns out it isn't you. Maybe it's someone else—or no one.

My leave from school starts soon, and in many ways not soon enough. Any focus that I had for work left me on March 29, when Randy came home from the hospital for good. Today I'm numb—no tears, just flat. It is what it is. I can't change anything, no matter how hard I try.

Last June, ten months ago, I thought Randy was dying. The cardiac arrest, the unresponsiveness, the ARDS, *the everything*. So we had another ten months together. Where did those months go? That's almost a year. How did the time go so quickly? I love this man so much. I'm still crazy about him, and now I'm going to lose him. What is my life going to be like without him?

April 22, 2012

A business partner from Charlotte, North Carolina, flies in tonight for meetings with Randy, current clients, and staff. I'm not sure how "up" Randy will be. He's slept a lot today, maybe in preparation for his meetings tomorrow? After reading the morning paper, he was back in bed by 10:00 a.m., and I finally woke him up at 4:00 p.m.

My brothers from Kansas drove out yesterday to see Randy. Both had asked when would be a good time to come, and I replied: as soon as you can, if you want to see him alive.

On April 30 Amy leaves for Ethiopia, for a court date for the adoption of Temesgen; she won't return until May 9. Jane and Brad leave on a trip to Kenya to see their children on May 21 and return on June 10. There is a brief window of time when both Amy and Jane would be able to be here: May 9 - 21.

April 23, 2012

I met with my pastor today to plan Randy's memorial service. Randy asked that she come to the house so he could give me "support" while I talked with her. However, he fell asleep shortly before she arrived and ended up sleeping several hours.

The service is planned. I need to find a current picture of him for the obituary in the local paper. We never took individual pictures, so it looks like I will be cropping one from a family photo.

April 25, 2012

Another day of the same stuff. Randy was up at 5:30 a.m. and back to bed by 8:00 a.m. for a couple of hours. My sister Marisa stayed with him during the morning so I could run some errands. He went back to bed at noon, and now it's 4:00 p.m. and he's still asleep. Yesterday and today he has had a lot of fluid in his lungs, but he has no energy to cough it up. He's talking very little as well. I noticed that with his business partner and staff yesterday he spoke little, and today he has said less. Is the fatigue morphine-induced or is it just the cancer? *Just the cancer*—what a strange thing to say. I ask him each time if he really wants his pain medication or not, and he always says yes. He had two bites of applesauce today, and that was it for the day.

Our new routine is that Brett comes over each morning around 6:00, before he goes to work, and stays with Randy while I take a two-to-three-hour nap. Randy and I are up several times in the night, and sleep is in short supply.

April 29, 2012

We hit another valley yesterday. I had given Randy quite a bit of morphine in the early morning because he couldn't seem to get any pain relief. He finally was able to rest around 9:00 a.m. When I checked on him at 11:30 a.m., his eyes were rolled back in his head, and he was struggling for air. I panicked. I called hospice and our kids. Randy was in and out all day. He has a different medication now that should decrease his mouth secretions.

May 2, 2012

More restlessness and up during the night many times. The night of April 30, Randy was up from 10:00 p.m. to 6:00 a.m. My kids are helping me by being here and letting me take naps during the day. But last evening, I lost it. Too many times of Randy trying to take off his clothes and his oxygen, and not understanding what I was saying. I was yelling at him and crying at the same time. In the end he patted my shoulder, but never said a word.

    I called my sister because I knew I couldn't trust myself. She stayed the night with him while I slept upstairs. Today I called an agency to have a nursing assistant stay with him at night so I can sleep. The assistant will be here tonight. I'll still need to give him his medications, but that's okay. I feel relief about the decision to have someone with him at night.

    Randy's feet and knees have some mottling. Mottling occurs near death as blood circulation decreases. The skin becomes purplish/bluish in color, and most typically begins in the feet.

May 5, 2012

I don't know how he gets weaker every day, but he does. Brett and I got him to the bathroom this morning, and it did take two of us. He insists on getting up and walking there. It's amazing that he can urinate several times a day when he has had nothing to eat or drink.

He's done a lot of sleeping today. I guess I could say that every day. I told him after his last nap that we would watch the golf tournament from Charlotte when he woke up, but it's after 5:00 p.m. and he is still asleep; at least I think it is sleep.

I just cancelled a caregiver for tonight. She was asleep when I came down to check on him at 1:15 a.m. last night. All the lights were out, after I had told her to leave the lights on in the bathroom, and I scared her when I entered the room. I should have sent her home in the middle of the night. Why didn't I? The "old" Pam would have had her out of there in a minute, but I didn't. And it just meant that I was up every hour checking on both of them. She apologized profusely, but I had entrusted her with Randy's care, and she didn't fulfill her end of the bargain.

Is this really happening? Randy is slipping away quickly. I don't remember the last time he had anything to eat. I give him water through a straw now. I washed his feet today in a plastic tub, hoping that would feel good to him. I tried to put lotion on his back, but it was difficult with all of his bones sticking out everywhere. He is miserable, just sitting there trying to breathe, weak, with his eyes closed. He doesn't talk anymore and is confused. Why do people have to die this way?

May 10, 2012

My soul mate is gone. Randy started becoming unresponsive yesterday evening. He had slept all day, woke up around 5:00 p.m., and then went back to sleep. I couldn't wake him after that. Hospice had stopped by with some adult pads (he had been incontinent for a couple of days). His breathing was sporadic during the evening. Brett and Jane stayed the night, along with the new nursing assistant. I was up during the night checking on him, but I knew I would always find him in the same position.

I came down at 5:00 a.m. and crawled into bed with him. His breathing and the mottling on his legs became progressively worse during the day. Randy took his last breath at 1:55 p.m. today. All three kids—Brett, Amy, and Blake—were here, along with Karrie, one of our daughters-in-law; Randy's sister Jane; and Martha, his mother. Oh, how I love that man!

Reflections

Randy's last six weeks of life were a blur. I had become increasingly irritated with his hospice care, but was unable to do anything about it or apparently even write about it until after his death. Writing in the journal during this time became nearly impossible. But some things are engrained in your thoughts, such as his brilliant mind becoming confused. His lack of drinking or eating. Not being able to talk. Randy asking me, "Am I dying?"

I wonder now, what is a peaceful death? Isn't that the goal for everyone? How would one really know? It would be your loved one's definition of a peaceful death, not yours as a caregiver. But there is no chance to ask.

On the morning of May 9, he kissed me back.

Widowhood

*I'll tell you;
I'll be bold.
You cannot know what this is like.
I don't want you to know
firsthand. But do not dare surmise …*

–Shelly Wagner, "Your Questions"

May 16, 2012

It has been nearly a week since Randy died, and I still cannot believe it. I miss him so much. Everything I do reminds me of him. I was okay for a while this morning, and then the tears came. I know this will continue for some time, but the hurt that accompanies the tears is overwhelming.

I picked up copies of his death certificate today. Shouldn't that make his death seem real? I see the memorial service book, the cards, and copies of the obituary lying on the table. Isn't that proof? I prayed so hard the last week of his life that God would take him and not let him suffer anymore. He was restless, confused, unable to eat or drink, incontinent—and now I want him here, no matter his condition. I want to hold him again.

I remember, again, that he kissed me back on the morning of May 9. I had come downstairs after the nursing assistant left at 6:00 a.m., and I did as I always did: got into bed with him, hugged him, told him I loved him, and kissed him. His only response that morning was that he kissed me back. I'm sure of it.

May 14, the day of Randy's memorial service, was a perfect day with few clouds, sunshine, and a temperature around seventy-five. The graveside service was at 10:00 a.m. Only family were invited to the burial. Retrospectively, I counted and believe that there were fifty-five family members there plus my pastor. But maybe I forgot someone. The service wasn't very long, maybe fifteen minutes. My pastor read some scripture and said a prayer, and then my kids, my grandkids, and I each placed a long-stemmed yellow rose by the box that held his ashes. Yellow roses were our flowers.

All family members were invited to my sister Marisa's house for lunch. Lots of good food, and the day was perfect for eating in the backyard. With so many family members present, many pictures were taken. Afterwards family met in the parlor of my church at 1:15 p.m., and the service was at 1:30. As I walked down the center aisle, followed by Brett, Blake, Amy, and then all the other family members, the church seemed full.

Brett's eulogy for his dad was amazing. I don't know how he got through it. I had talked with Brett the night before, and I knew that he was still writing it. I had told him that he didn't need to do it, and he responded, "That's my job. I'm the oldest. Mom, you did the eulogy at your mother's service, and when I asked you why, you said, 'Because I'm the oldest and that's my job.'"

The eulogy was followed by a slide show. We had all worked to find pictures of Randy from birth until the present, and what Karrie was able to put together was beautiful. I was thankful that I had seen the finished product the night before to prepare myself.

There was a reception in the fellowship hall of the church after the service. I was told that the line was very long, and that some people chose not to wait. And after looking at the guestbook, I realized that there were a number of people at the service I had not seen at the reception. Perhaps the biggest surprise was seeing Dave, one of Randy's former partners who now lives in Edmonton, Alberta. I had called Dave a few weeks before Randy's death; he and Randy were able to visit on the phone.

The gathering of family and friends continued from the reception to our house—now *my* house. Kareen, Amy, and Karrie did a fabulous job with food and drink.

May 20, 2012

I was going to write on May 17, one week after Randy died, but somehow I couldn't do it. Writing in my journal makes it more real, and I don't want it to be real.

So now it has been ten days since his death. I still feel numb. I feel like he is in the other room, at the office, on another trip. How could these last six weeks have gone so quickly? We thought we would have a couple of months of a normal life, maybe more, but we had maybe a week before he started to decline. And then it seemed like every day there were new things he couldn't do. The most upsetting thing, among many, was his inability to talk during the last three weeks. His partner from Charlotte came that week in April, and later that day he talked with a close friend, and then the words stopped. His speech was limited to single words: bathroom, wheelchair, cold, pain, up. And then it was nodding his head, and finally, in the last week, he didn't speak or nod at all. It seemed that as soon as his business with his firm was finished, he quit talking.

When did the terminal restlessness begin? I don't even remember. All of a sudden he was getting up twenty times per night to sit in the chair, sit on the side of the bed, move to his chair in the living room, go to the bathroom. I was with him every step of the way because he wasn't safe by himself anymore. Sleep became elusive for both of us.

May 29, 2012

Perhaps I should have chronicled each day since Randy's last dismissal from the hospital, but I was too caught up in each moment. Every day I was busy taking care of him. His last drive was to go to the cemetery with me to buy our plots.

If I thought that the six weeks between discharge from the hospital and his death were a blur, the same can be said of May 10 through 29. Randy has been dead for nineteen days. Just writing the word "dead" is hard to do. Can this be so? We had lots of talks about dying, death, and memorial services, but that was pretend. It wasn't real. We both knew when he was diagnosed that he was going to die too soon. But somehow you always think that you will be the exception.

June 4, 2012

I am at wheat harvest in Kansas with my brother Doug and his partner Judy. It was a hard decision for me. I was afraid to leave town. Somehow I felt like I was leaving Randy. Although his presence is overwhelming in the house, and you would think I would want to get away from the grief, I feel close to him there and didn't want to leave. The night before I left for harvest, I felt terrible—lots of tears and thinking that I had made a bad decision. Somehow, the next morning I got in the car and headed east to Kansas, crying for the first two hours. I'm okay now, although I feel that the tears are right below the surface most of the time.

How long will I stay? I'm just taking it day by day. No promises, although I'm thinking that when the equipment moves to the land north of Rozel, it would be a good time to leave. I just want to be back in my own house. There is comfort in that. I still think of him every minute of the day. His image is in front of me constantly.

June 5, 2012

I'm leaving in the morning to see my dad briefly and then on to see my sister Denise. I'll stay the night and leave the following morning for home. I made up my mind last night that it was time to go. I need to start working on my new normal, whatever that is. Interestingly enough, I got an e-mail today from one of the authors in my textbook, just asking how I was doing. I responded about Randy's death. Randy's death. Did I write that? It continues to feel pretend. What or when will be the turning point? When will I face reality? Or will I?

June 9, 2012

It will be a month tomorrow since Randy's death. I walked to the cemetery this morning with Amy. I saw Randy's name, date of birth, and date of death on the temporary marker. How can that be?

It's now nineteen months since his cancer diagnosis, and I can't yet wrap my arms around it. Did I think we were so blessed that nothing bad would ever happen to us? I don't have any answers, just questions. Why Randy? It just makes me sick to think of all of the treatments, hospitalizations, chemo, radiation, surgeries, more bad days than good days. We never had more than a month at a time of "good" time. He was never in remission. What an awful kind of cancer to have.

Living without Randy doesn't seem possible. We were together forty-seven years, married for forty-three. Last week, when I was on the college campus where we met, it was hard to think of not being there with him. The memories I have of that school are all associated with Randy. I see our favorite places, but something doesn't seem right. Randy isn't here.

Reflections

I still remember the first day we met in our freshman year of college. It was the day that I moved into my dorm room that would be my home for the next nine months. Mom and I had gone to the car, again, to bring more things up to my room on the sixth floor. We stopped briefly at the dormitory mailboxes and Linda, a new friend in the room across from mine, stopped to introduce Randy to me. They had met during a freshman orientation session over the summer. No, it wasn't love at first sight, but I remember our meeting vividly.

Within a week or two, a group of us—girls and guys, including Randy—ate most of our meals together in the dining room of the dorm. (Guys from the men's dorm ate meals in my dorm, the women's. This was long before coed dorms!) There were a couple of tables where we congregated, just a bunch of young adults laughing, talking, and being friends.

Oh, we each dated others in those first couple of months of the fall semester. Randy dated my roommate, and I dated Randy's best friend from high school, among others. Then one day I was walking to the mailbox on the corner to mail a letter—yes, something we did a long time ago—and ran into Randy on the sidewalk. We talked for a while, and he asked me out for the following Friday. I explained that I was going home for my high school's homecoming game and dance. Somehow we decided that he would come to the game and dance with me. He would stay the night with one of my high school friends whom he knew from his dorm. I remember this all as if it were yesterday. How I would love to relive those years, both the good times and the bad times.

We were crazy in love by the spring. I don't know how or why, but I knew I had found my soul mate. By the following summer we were talking about marriage, although that couldn't happen for years. We loved each other and truly believed that we were meant for each other.

During our sophomore year Randy decided to major in architecture, as he had wanted to do from the beginning. Our school didn't have an architectural program; it was mainly a teacher's college and liberal-arts college in those days. So Randy transferred to the university the summer after our sophomore year. I hated to see him go, but he was pursuing his dream career, just as I was pursuing mine in nursing. We were 170 miles apart, but our love never wavered. We were engaged at Christmas of our junior year and married in March 1969, the day after I finished the nursing program. And as they say, the rest is history. We were partners, soul mates, lovers, best friends.

So as I look around the campus and see our dorms, our walking paths, the bridge over the creek, the science building where we met after class every day of our freshman year, the student union—it is our campus. Such fond thoughts come to my mind as I think of our first two years together on this campus.

June 16, 2012

I wonder "where" Randy is? I'm obsessed that he didn't believe in God or heaven. I pray every night that God will wrap his arms around Randy, but is that even possible? I want so badly to see him again when I die.

I don't have any dreams about him. Why? I want to see him again, if only in a dream.

June 23, 2012

I'm at the cabin with my sisters, Denise and Marisa. We just had an evacuation (voluntary) for the nearby Waldo Canyon wildfire.

Last night we went to Randy's and my favorite restaurant. How many times had we, as a couple, been there? Too many to count. There are so many firsts, and last night was one of them. The music at the restaurant tonight was all late 1960s and early 1970s. I started crying. It reminded me of all of the years that we spent together. How many times can I say, *I don't believe what has happened.*

I want to feel okay about where he is. Where is that? I want some kind of sign that he's safe so I don't need to worry about him. How could such a huge chunk of myself be gone? Being at the cabin without him—how can that be? I want to wrap my arms around him.

I remember again when Randy kissed me back the day before he died. I went in to say good morning and tell him that I loved him, and I kissed him. He kissed me back: Wednesday, May 9, 2012, at 6:00 in the morning.

I don't remember him moving again after that. He had started to become incontinent that morning. We had been left with these giant adult diapers for a man who weighed 120 pounds. His hospice nurse was busy and couldn't come that day (*why?*). I got a call around 6:00 that evening from the on-call nurse asking if we wanted her to stop by. Yes, we did. She examined him, especially the mottling on his legs, and left us with the appropriate-size pads for his incontinence. Why can't I remember more of his last full day alive? But then, he wasn't really alive that day.

June 30, 2012

I still try to remember things from the last few weeks when he was alive. I wrote in my journal so sporadically then, too busy with caregiving to worry about a journal. But now I wonder: When did he last eat? When did he last talk in sentences? When and what was his last word? Why didn't I send that nursing assistant home in the middle of the night when I found her asleep while caring for my husband? Why didn't I complain to hospice about Randy's poor care? It was apparent early in his care that his nurse and nurse's aide weren't very good. One day after he was unable to brush his teeth independently, I asked him how the nurse's aide was helping him. He said, she doesn't brush my teeth anymore. Isn't oral care basic? And the inappropriate comments by his nurse were very unsettling. Everything that hospice did was reactive to what was happening. What happened to being proactive and anticipating what Randy and I would need? That's the job of hospice. I realize that as a nurse myself for many years, I have very high standards. But the "old"

Pam would have called hospice and asked for a different nurse and nurse's aide. My only answer, and it is a poor one, is that I was tired and frightened, and I didn't have the energy to face more change. I would have had to be courageous to complain about his nurse. I wasn't feeling courageous. The cancer journey had taken much from me. So I did nothing.

How am I doing? How should I feel? Since grief is such an individual feeling, I don't know. Sadness permeates my being. I don't cry as much now, so is that a good sign? The evenings continue to be my worst times of the day.

I'm headed back to work on Monday, and I don't want to go. It doesn't even seem remotely like something I want to do.

July 7, 2012

I'm at the cabin for a few days. It has been lovely. I think of the good times Randy and I had here, and also about the crummy ones. I thought it would bother me to be here without him, but nothing is worse than being at home without him. I've done some quilting and lots of reading.

I went to work this past week for two days. It was good to see friends there. I have moved my office to another space that I will share with someone else. I'm only working half-time this year. Work is okay, but right now it's a place that I don't want to be. Everything I do seems like I've done it a million times before. No challenges—but then, I don't want any challenges. And there is the ninety-minute commute to school. I will teach this fall, and in the spring will do special projects for the school. What will I do after that? I need to do what's right for me (whatever that is) instead of feeling guilty about letting Mary, Sue, and the School of Nursing down.

Our family spent July Fourth at Amy and Shane's house with the whole gang. I brought Grandma, the other widow in our family. We had a nice supper and visit and left early. Then I bawled my eyes out when I got home. Randy wasn't there.

The loneliness is overwhelming. I have people all around me, but he's not there. This coming week, it will be two months since his death. In some ways it feels like Randy died a long time ago, and in other ways it was only yesterday. How do people live through this? Couldn't Randy have been in the fourteen percent who live five years with esophageal cancer? Why not?

July 16, 2012

I read what I wrote last night, and the tears well up in my eyes again. The last few days have seemed almost worse than the first month after he died. Most days I want to scream and cry at the same time, just like when he had cancer. Why did he have to worry about his damn architectural firm during his last few weeks? I'm bitter that his firm took his last bit of energy. This firm will be down the tubes in nothing flat without Randy. No work, no marketing, no jobs for his employees.

Why didn't I make that nursing assistant leave as soon as I caught her sleeping when she should have been caring for Randy? Why didn't I ask for a different hospice nurse? Why can't I remember when Randy last talked? Last ate? Last had anything to drink? Why?

July 18, 2012

Lots of tears today. Is it because it's close to Randy's birthday? I don't know, but I feel lousy. Tears just below the surface at all times. Randy's image is in front of me all the time, even when I'm busy. This coming Monday he had planned to be with his sons playing golf at Pebble Beach for his sixty-fifth birthday. Then we moved the trip up to April, and then, in the end, he was even too weak to go to the cabin.

I finalized my letter to hospice today. It took a lot of emotional energy. But I want the letter off of my "things to do" list. Will it bring closure? No. I will continue to have what-ifs regarding Randy's hospice care. I suppose I will always feel guilty about what I did and didn't do. I'm hard on myself, but that's the way I've always been.

I was planning on going to work tomorrow, but I can't do it.

July 20, 2012

I mailed the letter to hospice yesterday. I have no idea what kind of response I'll get.

I'm constantly ruminating about something I should have done for Randy or shouldn't have done. It is so hard to understand how I will ever feel better. There is the acute sadness and then the long-term sadness and heartache. I've thought of suicide in very broad terms. Suicide—there, I've said it. I've put it on paper instead of just thinking about it. I've had dark thoughts like these off and on for a number of years. Randy knew about them. Maybe my medications aren't right or maybe grief has to hurt this badly.

July 23, 2012

Today is Randy's sixty-fifth birthday and also the day he was to fulfill his dream of playing at Pebble Beach. I guess his final hurrah with golf was his Phoenix trip in March with his golfing buddies. This day is also nearing his planned retirement date of July 31, 2012. Something he never got a chance to do: retire.

I took flowers to the cemetery this morning and then tried to do things around the house until I picked up Marisa for lunch. Our family physician (I guess he's just mine, now) called after my walk to the cemetery. He asked how I was doing, and I was crying and saying not very well because it's Randy's birthday. "I know," he said. "That's why I'm calling you."

Just a day of remembering and crying. I talked with Juli, one of Randy's cousins, for an hour and then Jane as well, but the tears keep coming. I can't describe how much I miss him. Will this ever get better or even livable?

July 27, 2012

I've almost made it through another week without him. My expectations are low, so making it through another week is all I can ask for. When I went to the cemetery on Wednesday, Randy's permanent marker was up. Somehow it made me feel better to see it instead of a temporary plastic marker. How unreal this is. The summer Olympics start tonight and Randy would have been glued to the TV, mostly for the track-and-field events. I love you, Babes, always.

August 3, 2012

I finally had a dream with Randy in it last night. I don't remember what it was about, but he was in it. It was the pre-cancer Randy, which was good.

August 5, 2012

Randy's cousin Delbert died yesterday of lung cancer. I am thinking of his wife. I know how she must be feeling.

August 9, 2012

I'm in a very down state now. Tears are frequent and seem to go on forever. Am I finally facing reality that he's gone? This bigger-than-life person is really gone? I think that Delbert's dying triggered something in me. Thoughts of more cancer, more death. I had planned to go to Nebraska to Delbert's funeral, taking my mother-in-law with me. The night before we were to leave, I backed out. Everything was too fresh in my mind from Randy's death. I couldn't make myself go.

    I got rid of Randy's underwear and socks this week. I didn't have any emotional attachment to those clothes like I do with others. I know the sadness will be here forever, but I am hoping that, somehow, it will lessen so I can function more normally again.

Reflections

The first three months after Randy's death passed quickly. Perhaps not each individual day, but the months. I wrote sparingly during that time, and now I don't even remember much of it. I consider my lack of memory of that period of time a good thing. The first family get-together after Randy's death was Memorial Day. I remember it now, but I didn't write about it in my journal. Panic was what I felt when I went to my son and daughter-in-law's house that day. I was scared. I didn't want to be there by myself and kept looking around for my partner. I was lost and left early.

I thought that by the end of three months, my tears would lessen. I was wrong. There is no timetable for tears—not then, and not now.

August 14, 2012

I received a letter back from hospice, finally. I need to close that chapter. Not sure the letter said anything: yes, we will look into his records, we'll further educate our staff, we're sorry that you thought your husband's care was substandard, etc.

How do I feel? Am I better? What is "better"? Sometimes I think I'm losing my mind. Sometimes I wish I were dead so I wouldn't have to experience the pain. I sit here tonight on the deck, still in disbelief. He should be here on the deck with me. Dead is not coming back, as in ashes to ashes, as in never seeing him again. My heart has this huge hole in it. I want to crawl into that hole and never come out.

August 17, 2012

I'm at the cabin, and I imagine him sitting in "his" chair as I'm curled up in the loveseat or recliner. I imagine the two of us in this room, together. But it's all imagination. I can't feel his presence at the cabin or any other place. I want to feel him somewhere, but I never do. There is just loneliness instead. We were such independent people, but we were interdependent as well. There is a hole in my heart that nothing seems to touch.

August 20, 2012

Today I sent an e-mail to my kids about talking about Randy. I think they all avoid talking about Dad because they're afraid they will upset me. But I need to talk about him and hear others talk about him as well. Otherwise, I feel like he is gone and living only within me.

Sometimes I just feel like a mess. Lately it doesn't seem like I have any good days. I feel the same way I did when cancer invaded our lives: overwhelmed, exhausted, and teary. I feel like I'm going downhill. Do I need counseling? I'm not a "group" kind of person; it would have to be a one-to-one situation. Don't I have a right to feel awful? We were together forty-seven years—almost half a century. Randy, why can't I feel your presence? I want to so badly.

August 28, 2012

I need to give up these thoughts:

1. I should have asked for a different hospice nurse, but I didn't.
2. I should have called the medical director of hospice for something other than Haldol for Randy's terminal restlessness.
3. I should have sent the nursing assistant home during the night after she fell asleep caring for Randy.
4. I should have gotten help at night sooner.
5. I should have gone on leave on March 29 when Randy was discharged from the hospital, instead of in mid-April. What kind of superwoman did I think I was?

6. I should have written more in my journal during those last six weeks of his life. Then I would have answers to these questions I haven't been able to let go of. When did he stop eating? When did he quit talking? When did the terminal restlessness begin? Why wasn't I more proactive to find a drug that would help his terminal restlessness?

August 30, 2012

The what-ifs and the should-haves. I'm sure there are more than I listed. They're so hard to give up.

And then there are other things I don't understand. A female friend of ours talked with Randy on the phone maybe three weeks before he died. I heard the last part of the conversation, his saying, "I probably won't be here when you come back." I've never heard from her and it's August. I think of the Charlotte office. Several folks had worked with Randy since 2001, including one of his partners. I never heard from them after his death. I heard from four or five former employees of the firm, but not the current ones. How crappy is that?

I called today to see a hospice grief counselor next week. I've decided I'm not doing this by myself very well, and I am tired of burdening my kids and sisters with my grief. Why did I decide to see a counselor now? I'm sure I will be asked that. Is it because I seem more teary than a few weeks ago? Maybe I'm more sad? My heart hurts more? The reality has set in that I will never see Randy again? I know that it is "'til death do us part." But I don't feel that way. He was everything to me: best friend, lover, husband, soul mate, my self-confidence booster. Now I feel that I don't have the self-confidence or the courage to do anything. I had to take an antianxiety pill before I went to see someone today about volunteering. How lame is that? Randy told me I could do things that I didn't think I could do. So what can I do without him? I don't have any idea. Often I think that I don't want to live without him. The hurt is too deep.

September 7, 2012

My first appointment with the grief counselor was this afternoon. It went okay, I think. Crying for eighty of the ninety minutes I was there makes one lose perspective. I did e-mail her the letter that I'd sent hospice in July, so she would have an idea of some of the issues I had with Randy's care.

My week has been okay. This morning I couldn't make myself do anything. No walk. I barely got through the newspaper. My grief counselor asked me what makes me feel better. I'm still thinking about that. Sometimes it is sitting by myself on the deck. Sometimes I can lose myself in a book. Being in the mountains, sitting by a stream, being around others … It's different each time.

September 13, 2012

For a few days after I saw the grief counselor the first time, I felt like a load had been lifted off my shoulders, that I could share my burden with someone else. Lately I just feel flat, no energy, making myself do things when I don't want to do anything. Why can't I just stay in bed one day with the covers over my head? I'm afraid it would become a habit.

I had a good day in the mountains with college friends. They've known Randy since grade school. We share a lot of memories of college and early married life.

Today someone at work said again, "You're so lucky that you have your kids and grandkids close to you," and of course I said yes, but I wanted to scream that it wasn't the same as having my husband here. I miss him so much and love him so much. Sometimes the pain is as bad as ever and sometimes not. Sometimes I really don't want to live without him.

September 19, 2012

I had a session with the grief counselor this past week. Is it making any difference? I don't know; if nothing else, maybe it's making me feel normal. We talked some about the letter to hospice. She feels that these issues have impacted my grief. As I look back at my list of things that I need to give up, several items are related to Randy's hospice care.

I've been talking and e-mailing with Susie, a friend since grade school. Her husband died five years ago. I have another friend whose husband passed away maybe three years ago, but our visits have often been depressing. I got cards from two widows shortly after Randy's death, asking me to call them. They even provided phone numbers, but I haven't called them. I can be bright and functional in meetings at work, but at other times I'm so flat that I don't want to be around anyone or do anything. Why do I have to keep telling myself that Randy is dead?

September 27, 2012

Just returned from a great three-day weekend with Juli and Jim (Randy's cousin and her husband) in California. But it is always good to be in my own house and bed. I need to address work stuff today, but I'd rather not.

Dead. Pam, why don't you get it? Why don't I dream about him? Why do I never feel his presence in a room or a place? I can't imagine what the holidays will be like. Some solicitor called last night for Randy. I was rude. I don't care.

October 3, 2012

Somehow I'm fixated on the idea of publishing this journal. Could our cancer journey help someone else? But as I reread my journal, it's so depressing. Wouldn't this be a downer book to read? Who would want to read a cancer story with a bad ending? But somehow, as a nurse, I want other nurses to understand what chronic illness is all about. I thought I knew, but I didn't. But who would publish something like this? Certainly not a traditional publishing company.

October 9, 2012

For the past four days, I've felt like I'm falling apart. The grief has been overwhelming, and I cry all the time. After returning from a nursing conference in Nashville, I felt like crying the minute I walked in the door. My grief feels fresh, raw, miserable. I saw my grief counselor today. Is it helping when I cry the whole visit? Today's crying started with the visit to the counselor, and now I can't turn off the tears. The future seems hopeless, and vague thoughts of suicide enter my mind again. Could I ever go through with it? No, not now, but I can see how easy it would be to give up. When I traveled last weekend, my flight was bumpy. Before Randy's death, I would have been petrified about crashing. But this time I was calm, because if the plane crashed, death would take away my pain.

October 15, 2012

I signed up for two hospice workshops. One is this coming Saturday; it's about art and writing, and will be facilitated by art therapists and a poet. It doesn't sound like me, but then I don't know who I am anymore. I also signed up for a journaling workshop for four Monday nights in a row. Maybe this can help focus my writing more.

Sometimes I really don't know what I'm doing. At lunch with an old teaching friend today, I couldn't keep the tears in check.

What is it like to be dead? Is Randy okay? Almost every night I've asked God to wrap his arms around him. Does that do anything? Can I live five years, ten years, or twenty years without him? I can't even imagine how. Lover, best friend, confidante, someone who always told me I could do it, even when my self-esteem was in the toilet.

October 17, 2012

I feel better lately, but I don't know why. I never know why. I was productive at work yesterday, followed by a homeowners' association meeting and then a chamber music concert. Today I'm cleaning my house with gusto. I'm thankful for a day when I feel normal.

October 20, 2012

A friend from North Carolina came this past weekend and the visit was great. This afternoon was my art and writing workshop on "weaving your grief journey." The first part was writing, something I love to do, but focusing was hard. There were many tears shed by the group, including by me. My art project, if you can call it that, was unique, but every part of it related to my relationship with Randy.

I'm tired of this hole in my heart. I'm mad that he's dead. He lived only eighteen months with cancer, and so much of that time was miserable for him. There was a lady at the workshop today whose husband died in the summer of 2010—and she's still going to hospice workshops? It was apparent that she was still very fragile, and she was mad that her husband had died. Will that be me in two years—still looking for answers that aren't there? Still feeling angry that life is unfair? Still hoping for what can never be again? This is why people think about suicide: the pain in your heart is so great that you can't think of anything else. Randy was my rudder, and I know he would say the same thing about me. Without my rudder, I seem to just drift along, going nowhere.

Reflections

I realized, when I looked back at this memoir, that I mentioned suicide several different times. That startled me and I began thinking about it.

Several years ago one of Randy's closest friends died of cancer. For several months afterwards Randy spent time with his friend's widow. She spoke of suicide on several occasions. I remember that Randy and I talked about those conversations, and both of us were shocked that this person would think of it.

Now I know how the pain of losing a spouse cuts to your very core. The knife in your heart turns and twists at will. You've lost your husband, your best friend, your lover, your everything. Can your heart ever mend? Can your life continue? Half of you is gone. It's then that thoughts of suicide creep into your mind. Death would take away the pain. Others might say that suicide is a selfish, cowardly act. But you're not thinking of others; you can only think of yourself, of finding a way to stop the pain. It's all about you.

October 22, 2012

The world doesn't understand the hole in my heart.

I really want to feel better. I try to visualize Randy: lying in bed with me, riding in the car with me, being by my side. Why do other people "feel" their loved ones and I don't? How can someone larger than life—to me, anyway—just be gone? Our whole retirement was ahead of us, and now nothing. Everything by myself.

All the perennials at the cemetery have been trimmed back for winter. It looks awful—just a berm of dirt with tombstones on it, ugly and barren.

October 29, 2012

I don't want to lose the words that I wrote at the "weaving your story" workshop last week, so I will add them here.

Octobers

I know it's October because I remember our first date on October 29, 1965, a mere forty-seven years ago. We were friends and just talked a lot, and then you asked me out, and we became more than friends. The innocence of youth, the energy that we bring to love.

It's fall, October; you are missing another season. First you missed summer and now fall. The leaves are turning and disappearing from the trees. And you aren't here. I think of our October days of watching grandchildren's fall activities, and watching college football together on Saturday afternoons and evenings. I think of our last October and walking around Bear Lake ... how hard it was for you and how long it took you, but then it gave us more time to enjoy the scenery and each other. I went to Bear Lake this October, yesterday, with a girlfriend, and we talked about life. How different, and it will never be the same again.

November 1, 2012

I look at the assignment for my hospice journaling class for Monday. I quickly jump over the prompt, "What gives you satisfaction now? What is the hardest?" I have no answers for these questions. I read another prompt: "Describe the person associated with your loss."

How do I describe the man who was my best friend? The person who said I was smarter than I thought I was, the man who gave me self-confidence and said I could do anything I wanted to, the man who fathered our three children and was grandfather to twelve?

From the outside he might have seemed stern, serious,

businesslike—and to be honest, he often came across that way. He opened his own architectural practice when he was twenty-nine. The peaks and valleys of the economy had always affected his practice. To others, he often seemed gruff. But his list of friends goes on and on. The tributes to him after his death were amazing, as people described how he had mentored them and supported them. Former employees since 1977 sent cards and letters and attended his memorial service.

The real Randy was quiet, humble, an introvert. He hated to market his business and ask for work because he was basically shy. He inherited a temper from his father, but over the past twenty years that had very much mellowed out.

He was a wonderful father to our kids. He demanded a lot from them and did his best to make them independent. As a result, shortly after college, they were all established in their careers and had strong, loving relationships with their spouses.

He was kind, he was funny, he listened, he understood the dark veil that descends on me every November and December. He followed me to two other positions, in Kansas and North Carolina, saying he had killed his giants and now it was time for me to do the same. We moved back to Colorado in 2006, and he opened a branch of the Charlotte architectural firm. He was a teddy bear at heart, but you had to know him to understand that. We talked in the last few months of how we were still just as crazy about each other as we had ever been. We realized that our relationship was one of a kind. I lost my best friend when he died.

November 2, 2012

I'm sitting on the deck in a sweatshirt and wrapped in a blanket, nursing a glass of wine just like Randy and I used to do. Even when it was cold outside, it didn't deter us from sitting on the deck. The deck was a special place for us—a restful place, a quiet place, our place. In the summer we would often read the papers here in the morning, and then in the evening settle in for some quiet time and talking.

The cemetery is barren now. I have a wreath for Thanksgiving that I will put at his grave next week.

November 4, 2012

I was looking for Randy's sweatshirt tonight. I usually wear it on the deck in the evenings. And in looking through some of his clothes, I found a sweater that he must have worn last spring. I picked it up and it smelled like him. Oh, what a heavenly smell. It felt good to know that his sweater still had his scent after all these months. Such a tiny thing, but reassuring. I wasn't sad. It gave me comfort.

Everything I've written in the last week or so in this journal seems so lame, just dumb stuff. I read it over, including my assignment for my writing group tomorrow, and it just sounds stupid. I don't know if all of this writing even helps me. I've lost my enthusiasm for publishing my journal. Who would want to read something that is so depressing, that ends in death and then widowhood? Who am I anymore?

I'm not sure why I'm at the cabin this week, a place that constantly reminds me of Randy. But Susie, a friend since grade school, is here and that's a good thing.

November 7, 2012

Instantly, when we were given our assignment in the hospice writing group, I was drawn to the prompt "what we smell" and how smells may dictate what we feel. Yesterday I left for the cabin, eagerly awaiting the smell and feel of the mountains. I sit on the deck, feel the calmness of the mountains and take in the smell of the pine trees. The birds are ever so softly chirping. Not a cloud in the sky, sixty degrees and gorgeous here at eight thousand feet. I feel peaceful sitting here as the sun warms my back. There's a deer ten yards away, quietly nibbling on grass, alone, not with his usual group of friends.

The community church in the village has a Bible verse on the front interior wall of the church that says, "The mountains shall bring peace to the people." And that is what I feel when I'm here. This is the fourth time I've been at the cabin since Randy's death, but the first time that I can feel the peace of the mountains giving me strength.

November 11, 2012

A few days before my birthday, my kids and grandkids gave me a wonderful party for my sixty-fifth. I am so blessed to have such great kids and grandkids. I'm still feeling the peace of the cabin and the mountains. It is a good feeling.

November 12, 2012

The writing prompt from my journaling class asked that I write a letter from Randy to me. What would Randy tell me if he could?

> Hon,
>
> You are such a strong person that I have no doubt you will make it through the grief much better than I could do. You always doubt yourself and have so little self-confidence in your abilities, but I have always believed in you and what you can do. You can do this! Since you always took care of our finances, that certainly isn't an issue for you now that I'm gone. I wonder if you are going to the cabin. I asked you that once last spring and you said that you would continue going. I hope you are doing that. Remember when we first built the cabin and we decided that we would just buy out your siblings' interest in it and live there forever? I asked you in the spring if you were going to keep my BMW, and you said yes, as you loved the race car almost as much as I did. You have lots of support from family and friends. Please lean on these people. Don't try to do this "grief thing" by yourself. I love you, Babes.
>
> Rel

November 15, 2012

Today is my sixty-fifth birthday, and you aren't here. How I miss you. The hole in my heart is so open today. The tears are less—a lot less—but sadness envelops me like a cocoon. My day was wonderful, with lots of e-mails, cards, and texts from family and friends. Tonight the kids surprised me and took me to Jay's for my birthday. We talked and laughed and had a great time. But you weren't here, my husband, lover, best friend, and you won't be here next year or the year after that either. Please make this pain lessen, Lord.

November 20, 2012

Although there are still days that I feel like I can't live without Randy, there are more days that I think I can figure this out, being without him. How I'm going to do this, I have no clue. But life is a puzzle, and I hope that I can put the right pieces together.

It was two years ago at this time that Randy was diagnosed with cancer. I look back on my entry of November 23, 2010, when life went askew, when everything that we took for granted was in question: our planned retirement in 2012; health; quality of life; going to the cabin at the drop of a hat; deciding to go on a trip, somewhere, again on the spur of the moment. Gone with the simple words "You have cancer"—stage IIIB esophageal cancer, squamous cell type.

We knew we were underdogs in this fight, but somehow you think that your love will be all-powerful and bring you through it.

I remember writing in our Christmas card of 2010 that we were up to the challenge of cancer, that we could do this. But we couldn't win the battle. Even through the pain and suffering, Randy, you were trying so hard to beat the cancer. And then we began hospice care, and we knew it was over. We thought we would have three to six months, but in the end we had six weeks. By the third week at home, you seemed to give up. You said it hurt too much to eat. I don't know whether it did or not, or maybe you just thought that death would come sooner if you didn't eat. But in the end, did it really make any difference if you quit eating? No, it's just something I think about since I've lost you. It's one of the what-could-I-have-done-differently-to-have-you-live kind of thoughts. It's always the what-if game.

Randy was an agnostic, although he'd been raised in a Christian family and had participated in church and youth activities. As a couple, we'd always belonged to a Presbyterian church and had usually been active in it. But the truth remains that he didn't believe what I believed. So in my continuing quest to address every issue I can think of, I wonder where he is now. Where do the dead go? I pray every day that he is safe. I don't know what else to call it but *safe*. Lord, wrap your arms around him and keep him safe.

November 22, 2012

Happy Thanksgiving, Babes, wherever you are. I am so thankful that I had forty-seven years with you. No, it wasn't enough and never will be—but our relationship was strong, we loved each other immensely, and we were always best friends.

November 23, 2012

It is two years to the day that I started this journal, sitting in the first of many waiting rooms. Unfathomable, the events of the last two years.

November 26, 2012

The tears came again at work today. It was just an innocent conversation with a colleague and something triggered my emotions. I want to cry it all out, but there are always more tears left. How many times have I been told that grief is unpredictable? That should be my mantra. Just when I think I have everything under control, grief comes to the surface, maybe as a test to see how strong I am. I still try to make sense of my grief, but I can't. Can you die of a broken heart?

November 27, 2012

Today, as I struggled with my emotions, I remembered something that Randy and I always told our kids when they were growing up. When something happened that they didn't like, they'd say, "That's not fair." Randy and I would both say, get over it, life isn't fair. And now I find myself saying it: life isn't fair. I need to get over it.

December 2, 2012

I've felt better the last week or so. As usual, one never knows why. Typically December is one of my "dark" months, but I don't feel that way this year. I bought a new artificial Christmas tree today. Why? Was I trying to make a fresh start? Was it just impulse buying or retail therapy? The old one was fine, maybe four or five years old. It fit nicely in a recessed part of the dining room. The new one is much taller and needs to be in the living room.

It is hard at any time of life not to be unduly concerned with what lies ahead. And it's particularly hard if you're a firstborn, have a type-A personality, and are at or near retirement age. Since I fit all three categories, I have struggled to envision what my life will be like even a year from now.

Yesterday I remembered something from two or three days before Randy died. His facial features had begun changing. I never mentioned it to anyone, but he didn't look the same as he had. His nose, ears, and face seemed longer. They lengthened, somehow. To me it was very visible, but perhaps not to others. I knew his face better than anyone, so perhaps no one else even noticed it. Randy weighed 130 pounds when he was dismissed from the hospital, and by the time he died, I would say between 115 and 120. Is this a part of dying? Do facial features change before death? I have been around a number of dying patients during my clinical days in the hospital, but I don't remember this. I was with my mother when she died, but I don't remember this change. Why would his facial features change in the last forty-eight hours of his life? It was like he was disappearing in front of my eyes. Was that the plan?

Widowhood: not for the faint of heart.

December 8, 2012

Today I am planning the cousins' sleepover, without Randy. Since Randy and I returned to Colorado in 2006, we've had a Christmas sleepover for all of the grandkids together on one Friday or Saturday night in December. The sleepover has included special activities, movies, a special breakfast, games, and more, and each grandchild looks forward to sleeping in the basement with all the other cousins (now numbering twelve).

I remember vividly the last two sleepovers. In 2010 we knew Randy had cancer, and he was waiting for his first treatment. I remember the difficult time he had eating one piece of pizza. In 2011 Randy had just finished chemo after tumors had been found in his lung. Such a different sleepover this year.

My niece Darcy is helping me, since with twelve kiddos it is hard to do everything by yourself. Randy isn't here to be the disciplinarian when the boys get out of hand. Randy always made pancakes and "little smokies" for breakfast the morning after the sleepover. Darcy and I will do it now. The first Christmas season without him, the first of many more to come.

December 11, 2012

The sunrises and sunsets have been beautiful lately. Wisps of clouds and gorgeous pinks, oranges, reds, and purples. I'm often overwhelmed by this splendor in the sky, and because of that I wonder if Randy's spirit is somehow there in some way. I want his spirit to be somewhere, anywhere.

My Christmas decorations are minimal this year. My crèches, angels, and snowmen remain tucked away in their storage boxes. Of course, I have my new artificial Christmas tree. The grandkids' stockings are hung, wreaths inside and outside the house, poinsettias on the fireplace mantle, but it's little compared to the past. I haven't played any Christmas music in the car or in the house. I don't want to listen to it. And of course music from our era is still off-limits.

I boxed up most of Randy's clothes today for a charity pick-up. Maybe that's why I feel teary tonight. However, his flip-flops, running shoes, and slippers remain in their proper place in our closet. I guess it is my closet now.

If someone would have told us on our wedding day—March 29, 1969—that we would have forty-three years together, I'm sure we would have said, wow, that's great, forty-three years is a long time. But the forty-three years went by so quickly, and it was not enough time. I wanted to spend forever with him, and I feel cheated. Retirement was on the horizon for us with time for each other at last. But now that possibility is gone.

December 13, 2012

I bought another "widow" book today. I'm not sure why. Maybe I'm still looking for those elusive answers on how to get through grief and widowhood. I was buying Christmas gifts and eventually found myself by the grief/loss/self-help books. Maybe I think there is some magic in these books, and that someone has found a way to live through grief and widowhood. But there aren't answers. I do seem to have figured that out. Just as grief is unique to each individual, dealing with widowhood is as well. I know that it is up to me to make a new life, alone. But somehow you always think someone might know something that you don't, some secrets to widowhood.

Am I getting better, each month since Randy's death? Yes, without a doubt. But a part of me is scared of that. I never want to forget our life together, and I can't imagine how I could do that, but at some point you find yourself not thinking of him every minute of the day. He doesn't consume your every thought and your being, and you feel selfish and unfaithful to his memory. You become afraid that your memories will slip away, become blurry and just fade into the background. You know, intellectually, that won't happen. But when it's nighttime and you slip into your empty bed, that fear increases. You may fear that you will have a new life, a new normal life, without him.

In the beginning, it doesn't seem possible that you could go forward. Every day is a trial, putting one foot in front of the other and plodding along. But for me, now, after seven months, I feel like I am moving forward. I've tried to figure out how this happened. Was there an event? Did I do something specific to cause this feeling? I look for answers, but there aren't any. Last Monday was the tenth of the month, seven months since Randy died. But I didn't remember the day as I had in previous months. This time I completely forgot about it until a couple of days later.

December 17, 2012

Randy and I always had coffee together as we read the morning papers, taking turns getting coffee refills for both of us. This morning I got up and poured two cups of coffee, just like in the old days—one with cream for me and one black for Randy. Why now? I have no idea.

December 19, 2012

I just finished the last "widow" book I will ever buy. I enjoyed the first part and could relate to it. However, the last part seemed to be written by someone from an earlier era. When the writing went to advice, I wanted to gag: congratulating yourself for writing your first check, making a decision, fixing something around the house. I need to stop buying these books. I'll have to find answers within myself. The answer I want is to go back in time and have the life we had before. That's the answer I want. But I can't; that life is over.

Every time I say or write the word *widow*, I think what an ugly word it is. I think of black widow spiders, the ones with the red spot on their backs. Is that how widows look? Do we have some kind of mark on us that labels us as such?

I'm reminded of when I was in the third grade, and I thought I had been bitten by a black widow spider. My kindergarten-aged brother and I had found some rock formations on the side of a hill near the football stadium several blocks from our house. Times were different in the 1950s, and particularly in a town of three to four thousand. We were on our own, exploring and loving every minute of it. My brother and I returned to the same place we'd been the week before, convinced that we had seen stalagmites and stalactites along with a glove that we had first thought was a human hand. This time there were many insects among the rocks, and one bit me. My brother and I were convinced it was a black widow spider. We ran home as fast as we could. For whatever reason, instead of showing the bite to my mother, I hid in our playhouse and cried. Eventually my brother persuaded me to come out and show our mother. I don't remember what she said, but she didn't take me to the doctor, so obviously she didn't think it was a serious spider bite.

Do we hide, as widows? Afraid to come out? Afraid of having to listen to thoughtless comments by others? Our home becomes a safe zone. Even though the memories of our loved one exist everywhere, home could be considered a place to hide. At home we can avoid the grocery store cashiers who say, hope your day has been grand and have a good evening. You want to scream, *How can I? I buried my husband last week, last month, last year. Why is everyone so cheery?* But they have no idea about your life, your feelings, the hole in your heart. It's not their fault, but it gives you another reason to stay at home, in hiding. Anything to avoid the pain.

December 20, 2012

I had a full-body massage tonight at my favorite day spa. As I was lying there trying to relax, my mind wouldn't turn off. I kept thinking about touch, or the lack of it, as a widow. How I long for touch, for a hug. I don't mean intimate touch—although I miss that as well—but the holding of hands, the hugs, cuddling in bed. Gone, all of it. I think of all the years that Randy and I shared, and his touch that I took for granted. I can't bring it back.

December 22, 2012

I'm having a pity party tonight, missing Randy and watching *It's a Wonderful Life* like we always did at Christmastime. As expected, I cried. Just thinking back on all of the Christmases we had together and the memories run together. I have no words tonight, nothing that expresses how I feel. Although the hole in my heart had closed slightly during the past month or two, tonight it is wide open and aching.

December 25, 2012

The end of a wonderful Christmas day with my kids, my grandkids, and my father. This is the first of many without Randy. How he would have loved this evening's long, spirited Trivial Pursuit game with the guys against the girls.

Merry Christmas, hon, wherever you are. I love you and miss you.

December 30, 2012

Randy's mom's ninetieth birthday party was a success for all yesterday. To think she has lived to be ninety, when her husband died at seventy-four and her son, Randy, at sixty-four. But then the first-graders at Sandy Hook Elementary School will never see second grade. God, how does any of this make sense? How can this be a part of any kind of plan for your creation? Or maybe there isn't a plan.

Christmas decorations are put away and another holiday passes without Randy. We've passed another season as well, now that it's winter. I hate this count toward the anniversary of his death, but these markers of time—the seasons, the holidays—are ever front in my mind.

Reflections

Fall has always been one of my favorite times of the year, but this year was different. My grief ebbed and flowed throughout the fall, always unpredictably. The dark veil that descends on me every November and December didn't appear this year, but of course I had grief in its place. I made myself do everything possible in the spirit of the holidays, whether I wanted to or not. Perhaps I just wanted 2012 to end and begin a new year. I struggle now remembering Thanksgiving and Christmas of 2012. Maybe that's an unexpected gift.

January 2, 2013

A new year, a new start. What will this year bring? Last year at this time Randy and I made plans for road trips that we wanted to take: a trip to San Diego and Phoenix in March, Pebble Beach in July, the Canadian Rockies in August. We made other plans: exercising more, taking more time for ourselves, and on and on the plans continued.

But we also talked about the what-ifs. We already knew that the cancer was back and that the chemo had no effect on it. So as logical, rational firstborns, we developed a plan for that eventuality as well. Recently I read that plan, written neatly in Randy's architectural handwriting. I'd always known where the plan was, but I hadn't wanted to read it yet. We remained optimistic at that time and had renewed energy to fight the cancer. Little did we know that Randy would die in a little over four months.

So, what am I going to do in 2013? I seem to avoid writing anything on paper about the new year. If the last two years have taught me anything, it's that life is fragile and plans often go astray. Since Randy's death, I've purposely not made plans too far in advance. I've tried not to count on plans coming to fruition. This is very odd for me because I'm a planner, a list maker, and an organizer of my life, both professional and personal. Now, I think about an activity, a plan, whatever, for a long time before committing to something. *Is this the right decision? Why do I want to do this? What can go wrong with my decision?* Never, *what positives can result from my decision?* My confidence as a decision maker is not back to normal.

Although I think about many decisions for quite a while, I blew it on my living room furniture. Never buy new furniture within six weeks of your husband's death. Yes, Randy and I had talked about getting new furniture, but I'm still not sure why I did it, particularly given the less-than-quality outcome. The furniture was not in stock so I did not see it previous to its delivery. The sectional had a lower quality of fabric than I expected, the end tables were too small for the room, and the rug was a disaster, having to be replaced after a month. I don't want any surprises. I was never impulsive, but I'm even more cautious now.

Well, I'm still avoiding plans for 2013. Maybe another day.

January 6, 2013

A couple of weeks ago, I had a conversation with a friend about Randy's death. She was amazed that I had slept in the bed where he died—our bed—that first night after his death. My response was, why wouldn't I sleep in the bed? I was comforted knowing that he had lain there so recently. The sheets had to be changed after he died, but it was still our bed. I found a favorite sweatshirt that he wore every day, and I cuddled up with it. It didn't smell like cancer or death, but like Randy, my life partner.

January 7, 2013

Today I thought of a conversation that Randy and I had, perhaps four weeks before his death. I was giving him his oral morphine, and he said, "One day I'm going to ask you to give me too much so that this will all be over, and you won't do it." And I replied, "You're right. I won't do it."

Reflections

This wasn't the first time we had talked about an overdose to end Randy's suffering, but the talks had always been in vague terms and more joking than serious. During Randy's last few weeks, when he asked me to give him too much morphine, I wasn't surprised. I remember the seriousness of Randy's request: help this be over. But I couldn't do it. As a nurse, it would have been morally wrong for me to do so.

January 8, 2013

What do I want to accomplish in 2013? I'd like to ask, what do I want to do for the rest of my life? But I can't go there yet. I always want to have a plan, some structure to keep me on task. But for the last eight months, I've basically just gone week by week and sometimes day by day. Yes, I may have a plan for the next week or month, but I haven't held myself to it. If I change my mind, don't feel like doing anything that day, I just don't. I'm attuned to what makes sense to me in the moment.

Often, when Randy was sick, neither of us had a plan for the day. Our days were dictated by how he felt. Our plans had been disrupted so many times, so we lived in the moment. So unlike the people we were, but so like families living and dying with chronic illness.

Kalid, one of my kindergarten-aged grandsons, asked me today why I had two big pictures of Grandpa (one in my bedroom and one on my desk). I said because the pictures remind me of how Grandpa looked before he got sick, and because I love him and miss him, even though his spirit is in my heart.

Seeing Randy's picture reminds me to keep plodding along, to not quit on life. I still have my dark moments, but they are fewer in number. Living a life without him didn't seem possible six months ago, but I keep putting one foot in front of the other, trying to figure out who I am and where I am going.

January 12, 2013

I made a decision yesterday to self-publish this memoir, the one I started writing the day that Randy was diagnosed. I've been thinking about it for several months; I've looked at various independent publishing companies and websites and have bought books on self-publishing. Today I signed a contract with a publisher.

My story is common, ordinary, one that is acted out every day by thousands of people. Cancer diagnosis, treatment, complications, more cancer, palliative care, a decision for hospice care, death, and then the long road of widowhood. Our experience with cancer wasn't unique; others have similar stories, but remain untold. I wanted to tell the *real* story. No one tells of the pain as the family watches the downhill course of a husband, father, brother, and son. The silent, untold experience of family caregivers needs to be heard. And I had even more to tell: I've been a registered nurse since 1969, more than forty years of practice and teaching, and almost all involving chronic illness. This is my specialty. I know it, live it, breathe it. I thought I knew what this journey was about, but I didn't.

January 14, 2013

I've been pondering the terms "loneliness" and "aloneness" and how, as widows, we have some of each at different times. But my brain isn't working tonight, and the terms seem muddled, just as my life is muddled.

January 18, 2013

Enjoying the cabin with a beautiful sunrise coming up over the mountains to the east. The eighty- to one-hundred-foot blue spruce trees that surround the cabin are still, and each branch is clearly defined. What tales these trees could tell. I'm looking for my deer friends this morning, but there are none to be seen. I have named them A, B, C, D, and E. These five young mule deer are always together. I see their hoofprints in the snow around the cabin, but nothing else today.

I had a dream last night about Randy, or let's say he was in the dream. We were both much younger, sitting around a table in the house where we raised our children, trying to figure out a budget for Christmas gifts. Dreams fascinate me because mine never seem to make any sense, including this one.

It is now over eight months since Randy's death. I often recall the day he died, but I think of it particularly on the month anniversary of his death. Am I on a countdown until it has been a year? So at a year, what happens then? Our ancestors often talked of a year of mourning, but what did that mean? Do widows and widowers no longer have any excuses for not participating fully in life? More questions, no answers.

I was reading a book last night about memoirs and what is truth within those memoirs. I think I remember the day Randy died—but I was only writing minimally in my journal at that time, so do I? And is there a chance that it brings me more peace that I *don't* remember all of the details? Perhaps it is a good thing that my memories of the day are blurry. I have enough what-ifs over the eighteen months of his illness and the time since his death. I don't need more.

January 23, 2013

I read somewhere that surviving the loss of a loved one is its own kind of test. What does that mean? To see if we pass or not?

Telling our stories affirms the life of the one we have lost—the experiences we had together, the favorite family stories. To tell the story is also a way of moving our grief along and may contribute to our healing.

This is our story, Randy's and mine. Even though he has not been with me for some time, it is still *our* story, not mine. And this journal encourages me to tell it. I have found much comfort in expressing my thoughts, ugly as they might be. I can't explain why it helps, and I don't even try anymore. People ask me why I would want to publish this journal containing my personal thoughts. I hope, by doing so, that someone else may be helped by reading them. Perhaps others have similar thoughts and are afraid to express them. Grief makes you crazy at times, and you feel like you're losing your mind. I hope that my words, my thoughts, may put others' minds at ease so they understand that they aren't crazy, but are responding to loss in a natural way.

January 25, 2013

In my dreams last night I was in a department store of some kind, unfamiliar to me, and I was looking for a Valentine's Day card and present for Randy. All of a sudden in my dream, I realized that Randy was dead. I was awake instantly.

It had been a restless night—too many thoughts. Yesterday I

received word that a sibling of Karrie's has advanced cancer with only a glimmer of hope for a cure. That started the floodgate of tears about Randy. A year ago at this time he would have been finishing up his CyberKnife treatments. How optimistic we were then.

February 1, 2013

Some days are still hard to get through, and often I don't know why. Something jogs my memory, words a person might say to me. Or I won't even know what it is. Wednesday of this week was like that. It was a day when I felt fragile from the start. I had my usual ninety-minute drive to work, meetings all day, and of course the return drive home. By the time I got home, I was physically exhausted. Often when I feel that way, emotional fatigue follows, as it did that day. I started crying around 6:00 p.m. and continued off and on for the next four hours. Just me, my memories, and my tears.

As I looked back today over the first few months of my journal, I was struck by how many times I said, this can't be happening, it's a dream, it's not real. That is a thought I still have almost every day: that Randy isn't dead, and I'm not alone. For over two years now, the same lack of comprehension of the events continues. One of the reasons that I go to the cemetery is to see evidence of his death. I look at the marker and see his name, his date of birth, and the date of his death. I just stare at it like it's the first time I've seen it. I try to make sense of his illness and death, but my mind freezes up. There is no logic, there is no making sense of the situation. I try, but fail.

February 3, 2013

I wrote this piece in a grief workshop. I think everyone has some experience with the distressing ways people respond to your loss.

Things I Wish People Wouldn't Say

1. <u>You look so good.</u> I heard that phrase for the first time on the day of Randy's memorial service, and it continues to this day. So does that mean a widow shouldn't look good? Should a widow look like she has cried all day and have bags under her eyes and a red face? Yes, I did look that way a lot, even before Randy died, but I tried to look normal when I went out. I believe people think that saying someone looks good is a compliment, but somehow it doesn't sound that way. It sounds like I'm not grieving the way they think I should. It is what it is. Some days I have bags under my eyes from crying and I look tired, and other days not so much. I typically don't respond to the comment anymore.

2. <u>I know just how you feel.</u> Unless you have lost a spouse, please don't tell me that you know how I feel, and even if you have lost a spouse, your feelings and my feelings, though we will have some in common, are different. Grief is an individual feeling. The first time I distinctly remember hearing that phrase was one month after Randy died. My oldest son and I had attended a benefit golf tournament and luncheon for scholarships for a local community college. The community college was one of Randy's clients, and he had completed many projects for them. The president of the

community college spoke about Randy at the luncheon and told attendees that the community college was donating five scholarships in his name for the coming school year.

One of the administrative staff, whom I didn't know but had heard Randy speak of, came up to me and said, I know just how you feel. She went on to say that her eighty-five-year-old father had just died unexpectedly, and she was mourning his death. I wanted to scream, no, you do not know how I feel. I've lost my soul mate and best friend, and your husband is still alive. Your father lived twenty-one years longer than Randy. Unfortunately remarks like that continue, but I pay little attention to them anymore. It has taught me to be cautious of what I say to those suffering a loss.

Two weeks ago, a teaching colleague of mine died of cancer at fifty-eight. She had had breast cancer eight years before, and was successful in defeating it, at least for a time. In November the cancer came back with a vengeance and spread throughout her body. I had a chance to speak with her husband at a special time of remembering this colleague. I told him that I understood a little bit of how he felt because I had lost my spouse to cancer the previous year. But I also said that grief is very individual, and that even though we had both lost a spouse, our feelings would be different as well as similar. Later in the conversation, I added my mantra since May 10, 2012: *grief is unpredictable.*

3. <u>You are so lucky to have your kids and grandkids close to you.</u> Somehow people think that is the answer to my grief, or at least that's how I perceive their comments. Yes, it is wonderful that my kids are close and can support me, but

it doesn't replace a spouse of forty-three years. The kids can understand my grief to a point, but losing a father when you are thirty-five, thirty-eight, and forty-one is different from losing your spouse.

February 6, 2013

One of my readings for the day was about the fallacy of being brave and stoic after a loved one's death. The author referred to a friend who had told a new widow, "You were so brave. You didn't break down once during the memorial service." Is this supposed to be the goal, to keep our emotions hidden from others? What we should be doing is sharing our emotions with those we love and trust. A memorial service should offer an environment that provides safety for us as we grieve.

However, on the day of Randy's memorial service and burial, I didn't cry until much later in the evening. It wasn't a willful or conscious effort on my part to keep myself together. It just happened. In retrospect, I was numb. I was doing what I had to do with little thought as to what I was doing. I wasn't strong or brave; I was still trying to believe the unbelievable. I remember standing in the reception line after the service, with people telling me that I seemed to be doing so well and that I looked so good. Maybe sleepwalking in a dream is a better description of what I was doing. I couldn't share my feelings in front of all of those people. It wasn't safe for me.

February 12, 2013

As it nears Valentine's Day—a holiday that Randy and I never celebrated—the day takes on more importance this year because it's my first Valentine's Day without him. The ads, the cards, the chocolate, the hearts. I never realized that there was so much *stuff* for this day. I'd hardly noticed it before. Where is my sweetheart? Where is the one who holds the key to my heart?

February 18, 2013

I'm often struck with the small things that have changed since Randy died. Things that I took for granted. I teach at a university ninety minutes from my house. On that route through the mountains the weather can change quickly, and the road often closes due to adverse conditions. At the top, around 8,300 feet, the weather is unpredictable even during the summer. Every day, before I left school for home, I texted Randy and said "headed south," so he would know when to expect me—or send out a search party! Still, nine months after Randy's death, I have the impulse to pull out my phone to text him.

February 21, 2013

I sit here tonight, more than 250 days since Randy has been gone, and wonder why him and not me. My love for him cannot be measured, and I wonder again how I can go on living without him.

How does this feeling ever lessen? It should have been me. I should have had the cancer, not Randy. I don't understand, God. Help me understand why. The hole in my heart isn't getting smaller.

March 4, 2013

I got rid of all of Randy's clothes in December, and yes, I barely mentioned that event in my journal. I have no idea why not, because it was a big thing to me. It had such finality to it. For a hospice writing class that I am attending this spring, I decided to write about his clothes.

Clothes

I'm a rule follower and mostly I like to "stay inside the lines," or at least I've wanted to for the last couple of years. I see Randy's clothes in the closet and wonder if it's time to move them, give them away. I'm not sure. A friend tells me that she left her husband's toothbrush in place for a year after he died. No reason why, she says, but just in case his death wasn't real. Another friend still has all of her husband's clothes in the closet four years after his death. She finally parted with his underwear a few months ago, but that is all.

Three months or so after Randy died, I got rid of his shoes. He hadn't worn many of them since he became ill. But parting with all of them was too much. I kept his special shoes (at least they were and continue to be special to me): his slippers, his leather flip-flops, and his running shoes. Funny, I still call them running shoes even though he hadn't run for more than ten years. Vertigo was the culprit, and he never felt safe running again. These shoes sit where they always have, and I see them whenever I go into the closet. I'm comfortable with them there; I want them there.

His clothes, however, were a different matter. Since Randy weighed ninety to one hundred pounds less at his death as compared with his weight before cancer, I had a variety of sizes of clothing to deal with. Upstairs, I had the "fat" clothes from when he weighed over two hundred pounds, starched dress shirts from the laundry all neatly hanging in the closet with dress slacks of varying sizes. Downstairs in our bedroom closet were the "medium" and "small" clothes. I see the top-zip sweatshirt pullovers that I bought during his first hospitalization. He wanted his chemo port covered as much as possible even when it was in use. I see the increasingly smaller size of shirts, slacks, and jeans, including the one sport coat, sweaters, and shirts that we bought together in January before he died in May.

But still hanging are six to eight suits and several sport coats bought during the time he weighed 215, dust covering the shoulders, never moved nor worn since his diagnosis. These suits and sport coats were not the gentle reminder that he was gone, like the shoes, but a "hit you in the face" kind of reminder. I decided one day in December that I could not look at them anymore. I called my favorite charity and by the next day everything was gone. One would think that with a momentous decision like this, I would have thought about it for days before, but for some reason I just knew it was the right time. I still have a drawer of his special things, a sweater, T-shirts, his wallet, driver's license, his glasses. The sweater is special because it still smells like him. Somehow his scent has been maintained on this sweater for nearly ten months. I continue to go to that drawer every couple of weeks for comfort. I don't cry over his things, but they remain an important remembrance for me.

March 18, 2013

The tears flow. I'm trying to transcribe the words I've written in this journal over the last two and a half years into a written manuscript for publication. Words become a challenge to type. The words are personal; they hurt. The memories of something distant come rushing back. And I'm still alone. It is I, not we. It is mine, not ours. Randy and I had something together that was unique. Now what? The memories, of course—but today they don't seem enough.

March 20, 2013

I almost wish it hadn't been so easy to find details for this piece from a hospice writing class.

Before

Before, we felt that we were a blessed family.
Before, we thought that cancer happened to other families, but not to our family.
Before, we were looking forward to retirement and spending more time at our cabin.
Before, we had eleven grandchildren and now I have twelve.

Before, we had dreams for the future, and now I have other dreams, different ones.

Before, I prayed he would die during those terrible last ten days, when he was confused, not eating or drinking, incoherent. I knew how he would have hated to be that way because we had often talked about that possibility during his illness. And then when death came, I wanted him back even in that miserable state he had been in.

Before, in early April before his death on May 10, he talked with me about his morphine, saying, one of these days I will ask you to give me too much so that it can be over, and I replied, you know I cannot do that.

Before, we talked about our cabin, our kids, our grandkids, our plans, and now I talk about my cabin, my kids, my grandkids, and my plans.

Before, it was we, and now it is I.

March 29, 2013

The memories of last March 29 are vivid in my mind, but when I look back at my journal, the writing is sparse. Randy was dismissed from the hospital on March 29, our forty-third wedding anniversary, and hospice care began. I remember both of us thinking, okay, three to six months. We can go to the cabin a couple of times and have a bit of a life before his health declines. Yes, he had tumors in his lungs that were not treatable, but we thought we had a chance at some time together. People don't die of lung cancer in a few weeks. That's what we thought. But by the end of his first week at home, we shared our concerns with each other: things weren't going well. By the end of week two, it was clear that we wouldn't have the time together that we so desperately wanted.

There were a couple of times in those first two or three weeks when Randy became anxious or his pain was different, and he would ask me, am I dying? I would respond, yes, but not today. And his anxiety passed. However, there was one time, probably two weeks before he died, when Brett and I were helping him back to bed and he asked again if he was dying. But this time I only said yes, instead of "Yes, but not today." Why didn't I give my usual answer? I knew it wasn't going to happen that day.

Why won't these thoughts go away? They are so hurtful, and they bring me back to the should-haves. There are times, like today, that the should-haves rush in and fill my mind. Then the tears come again. When it comes to Randy, I can't forgive myself for anything I've said or done. I wanted to be perfect for him during those last few months, but I wasn't.

March 31, 2013

Easter Sunday. I am remembering last Easter Sunday, April 8, the Easter-egg hunts for the "bigs" and the "littles."

I took a picture of you, Randy, by yourself, on the deck. Kareen took one of both of us. You didn't feel good, I could tell, but you pretended you were fine. You were still able to walk by yourself then. You ate little that day. I know all the grandkids' boisterous behavior bothered you; we talked about it later in the evening. You were tired and not feeling well, but we were together.

April 2, 2013

Once upon a time, I couldn't imagine going to bed at night and not feeling Randy's warmth and closeness. And now it is gone. For a number of years, if one of us went to bed before the other, the last one to bed would move their legs over to the other's and intertwine them briefly. Since I was the early riser and Randy the night owl, typically it was he who came to bed later and would get into bed and rub his legs against mine. I may have already been asleep, but this movement awakened me a little and made me feel loved and safe. I'd fall back asleep easily.

And now I get into bed and automatically my legs search out his legs, but they're never there. It's cold on his side of the bed. The sheets are pulled tight, his pillow undisturbed. And I remember, again, that he is gone.

April 5, 2013

My life is what I am given now. We can't stop rearranging the facts to make reality different.

April 10, 2013

Does grief sometimes require new words? *Neverness*: for each of us with a loss, things and events that will never be again.

Where do I begin? Randy has missed so many things since he died last May. There are the obvious holidays and birthdays, but sometimes it is sitting on the deck together, enjoying a summer sunrise together, time at our cabin, or just a simple walk together—things that will never be. But the neverness that I miss the most is that he will never know his grandchildren, and they will not know him. We—I—now have twelve grandchildren from ages two and a half to eleven. Two families have five children and the third family has two children. The older grandkids, the ones in grade school, will remember Grandpa for now. But soon those memories will fade. The five younger ones, from age five down, will never remember their Grandpa Larsen and how much he loved and cared about them. Grandpa will be someone their parents talk of, but they won't be able to visualize him. My newest grandson, Temesgen, was ten when he arrived from Ethiopia in July, two months after Randy died. They will never know each other: Temesgen, a shy, quiet, eager-to-learn child from the Gambela region of western Ethiopia, and his Grandpa Larsen, my daughter's father.

The youngest children—the twins who are now four but were three when Randy died, and Lainey, who is now two and a half—often walk into my house and say, Grandpa is dead, and I say, yes, he is. They are verifying what they observed from last year and what their parents or big brothers or sisters have said. In many ways, I am verifying the same for myself: yes, he is dead. But it never seems real, and I don't want it to be real. We're still planning our trip to the Canadian Rockies for summer or we're figuring out how to relandscape our front yard or whatever. But it's not going to happen.

Never is a long time. I've made it nine months without him, and the nevernesses continue. Every day Randy misses something. Sometimes I can gloss over the event, but others are too painful and

I start to cry again. I've lost my way these last few weeks and don't know why. The tears are right below the surface and the lump in my throat is always there. I need to get my spirit back, but I don't know how. Grief continues to be unpredictable.

April 13, 2013

I sit here in the early morning as the sun is rising and remember our time together watching sunrises. Sunrises, something you never appreciate when you're young—but with age, their beauty becomes more striking. We'd be reading the morning papers together on the deck, and one of us would notice the colors in the sky, and we'd both stop and pause, enjoying the sunrise.

This morning the sky has shades of pink and purple with a few thin, wispy clouds streaking across the horizon, signaling a new day. Tears come to my eyes as I remember last April. I want to remember those last times together, but I already feel the details slipping away. Randy wasn't Randy anymore, but I keep hanging on to those memories in hopes of finding or recalling something good.

My sister-in-law Jane, Randy's sister, was here this past week. It was her first opportunity to see Randy's gravesite since the memorial service. She asked me if it bothered me to see my name and birth date on the grave marker. Truthfully, I responded no, not at all. It bothers me to see Randy's name there.

The deep pinks and purples of the sunrise—long ribbons of pink and then purple. I want to believe that Randy is a part of that sunrise or is a bright and shining star in the sky at night. I want his spirit to appear in something I can see and feel. The love I feel for him is so strong this morning. Since I can't feel his presence in this room, where I watch from the window, I need to feel him in the sunrise or among the stars or in a mountain stream.

April 14, 2013

Dear Randy,

There was an op-ed piece in the *New York Times* this weekend about a photographer following a dying man—not anyone the photographer knew, but a stranger. There were some pictures of the man at various stages of his illness. The photographer had wanted to see a "peaceful" death. I was surprised that the photographer was able to find someone who would allow his space to be invaded or perhaps even violated in some way. Death is an intimate experience. But my bigger question after reading the article was for both of us: Did you die a peaceful death? I want to say yes, that it appeared so to me, but I don't really know. You were not responsive for roughly thirty hours before you died, but were you pain-free? Could you hear us and were unable to tell us you were in pain? Could you feel us touching you, caring for you? Or had you slipped into another world already? Does a peaceful death mean that you aren't aware of what's happening and death comes? We—society, hospice—say that the goal is a peaceful death. Peaceful death sounds likes an oxymoron to me, but perhaps that comes from the struggle with my faith.

I remember that sometime during your illness, you and I talked about visiting a cemetery after someone dies. You told me that if

I died first, you'd never go to the cemetery. My spirit wasn't at the cemetery, so there was no reason to go. I, on the other hand, said I needed a place to go, that I would be at your grave on a regular basis. And I do continue to go there. Do I find comfort in doing so? Comfort isn't the word, but I feel compelled to go—something draws me there. As I've said in the past, one reason for my cemetery visits is to validate what I know is true: you died on May 10, 2012. The date of your death is always the same, as is your birth date. I *will* the date of your death to disappear, but it never does. I *will* my life to be as it was before, but that doesn't happen either. You're gone. And I wish again, pray again, that I will feel your presence, somewhere, somehow. I love you so much.

I continue to pray for your safety—isn't that weird? Every night I pray that God will wrap his arms around you and keep you safe. Safe from what? I don't even know what that means, but it is my nightly prayer.

Babes, I love you. It's close to a year since your death. At times it seems like yesterday, and at other times it feels like you have been gone a long time. I still imagine you opening the garage and coming in the back door. You're cooking, and I'm waiting to taste one of your many recipes. You would be appalled at my diet now: frozen dinners, food from the deli at the store, anything to avoid cooking. You were the cook while I was the cleaner-upper.

How many times a day do I think, *I need to tell Randy this because he needs to know, or he'll think it's funny, or he'll think that is so lame or...* But you're not there to tell. So I tell you these things in my mind. I'm always talking with you somehow, out loud or in my mind.

And that brings me to another issue: you are always on my mind. Sometimes I try to push you out so I can get work done, try to concentrate on other things, but I can't. At times I feel like my brain doesn't work at all; it's too full of you. When my mind is so full of you, I am paralyzed and can't do anything. I fall back into my pity parties. Why me? Why you?

People think I'm doing well—at least that's what they tell me—and to the outside world, I am. But there is an inner self that only you knew, and that part of me isn't well yet. Am I going to commit suicide? Do I have the dark thoughts that I had earlier? No, those thoughts are gone, thank goodness. But the person that you knew isn't here anymore. Maybe that self will come back, or maybe not. Maybe it can't come back. Your death has created a new me. I can't be the way I was with you anymore. I'm evolving into a new Pam, a different one. I prefer the old me with you at my side, but that's not possible. Who will I become? Would you like the new Pam? Would you love her? That is what I'd want.

Forever yours,
P

April 15, 2013

My meditation for today followed my thinking and writing of last night. With grief, one's life changes, and it is a mystery or a surprise as to what we'll become as we grow through our grief. I wrote last night about the new Pam, that I don't know how I will evolve. Today's meditation says it best: I don't know all that I may become.

May 2, 2013

I've avoided this journal as the countdown to the anniversary of Randy's death nears. Well, at least I think that is the reason. What am I expecting? Less grief, since the first year will have passed? A renewed spirit for life? Am I hoping that the second time through events, holidays, and meaningful dates will be easier, better? I don't know. As I talk with friends who have lost their spouses, it seems that many continue to have similar feelings during Year Two. Yes, the feelings may not be as intense for some (not all), but each individual is still marking time.

Tomorrow morning I leave for a trip to Pebble Beach with my three children. This is the trip that Randy wanted to take with his sons for his sixty-fifth birthday in July 2012. His dream was to play golf at Pebble Beach on his birthday. We tried moving up the trip to April 2012, after knowing his cancer had metastasized, but it never happened. So the four of us will make that trip tomorrow with Randy's spirit guiding us. The boys will play golf at Pebble Beach and Spyglass, and Amy and I will go to the spa and ride bikes. This was Randy's trip, not mine. But he didn't live to see his sixty-fifth birthday and realize his dream trip. So it becomes our trip, commemorating his death of nearly a year ago. I know in my heart that he would be happy that we are taking the trip. But there will be a void that can't be filled. Randy, Dad, my best friend—he won't be with us, but I await feeling his spirit on the trip.

May 8, 2013

Our commemorative trip to Pebble Beach was a success. I don't often get time alone with my grown children, and I feel blessed that I got a few days with them. It was difficult not to think of Randy every minute we were there, knowing how much he'd wanted to be there. And looking back on his desire to go, I see that it might have been more about reaching a goal, three to four months later, than about actually being at Pebble Beach. No one but Randy knows what it was to him. But Babes, we made your trip. The boys took some of your golf balls with them (the ones that you kept on your dresser) and ceremoniously hit them into the ocean for you. Brett put a Pebble Beach golf-bag tag at your grave upon our return. You were loved, Babes, always, and will continue to be. Your presence shaped each of your kids and me.

I was explaining our relationship to someone yesterday, and it was hard to describe this independent-interdependent relationship we had. I feel like we were joined at the hip since our first date in 1965. And now there is loss, and there are feelings I didn't know could exist. The hole in my heart is still there, and this week it is as wide and deep as ever.

May 10, 2013

Dear Babes,

A year ago today you left this life. At times I relive everything I can remember of those last few weeks, and then back to your diagnosis and then to our prior life together. Thankfully, my memory of your last few days has faded. They were hard ones for you and me. You weren't "you" anymore. The confusion, the inability to communicate—you would have hated being like that. Your brilliant mind gone, just a tiny piece of what it had been.

At times it seems like more than a year since you've been gone. It gets harder to remember things. For example, our road trip to California and Arizona in March 2012, or the wonderful time we spent at the cabin at Christmas 2011. I want to remember every detail vividly, but I can't anymore. I want to treasure each of those moments, but they have become fuzzy in my mind.

I think of so many events as either before or after the diagnosis. Our life became so different in the eighteen months of cancer. It was "before cancer" and "after cancer." And my life now has two distinct periods of time: before your death and after your death. Before it was *we*, and now it is *I*. It's hard to change *we* to *I*.

Your pictures sit on my dresser in the bedroom and on my desk in the kitchen, but your presence is everywhere. Just now I'm remembering the pasta maker and the crème brûlée torch, both yours, that I sold at my garage sale last year. Why those thoughts come into my mind now, I do not know, but such random thoughts of you still come. Yes, the big things and events still bother me, going to them without you. I worry about them in advance, cry about them, worry some more, and then they burrow into my heart, the heart that has a gaping wound in it. But the randomness of the small things, the memories of everyday life together—those thoughts just pop into my mind when I least expect them.

What have I learned during this first year without you? Grief is unpredictable. Loneliness is frequent even when I'm with someone else. The hole in my heart tries to close, but then something opens it up again. That our life together was amazing. That my love for you is deep and cannot be measured. That I still wake up every morning and think I will see you, somewhere.

It's nearly summer again, a full year that you've missed. I still cry, often at unexpected times. I was reading books to the youngest grandchildren last week, and suddenly the tears came and I couldn't stop then. But I've made it through a year without you. How I would love to have you with me, but I can't. Remember that you are always in my heart.

Love you,
P

Epilogue

> *I didn't plan to be this person, for whom loss hovers at the edge of my awareness... I've carried the remote ache of longing with me long enough to understand it's part of who I am now.*
>
> —Hope Edelman, *Motherless Daughters*

It's fall again, always a season of reflection for me. Since Randy's illness and death, seasons, instead of months, have become my markers of time passed. Seasons somehow encompass a whole, while individual months are only small snapshots of time. I look back at the two and a half years of my life reflected in this memoir and see the clarity of my thoughts at times—but much more often, confusion, fear, and disbelief.

A memoir can't and doesn't document everything, but as I reread the text, some things are clearly missing: events, decisions, feelings that were important to me but were never mentioned. It's odd, and I can't explain it. For example, I rarely mentioned the support that I received from my family and friends. This memoir makes it sound like I did everything on my own, but nothing could be further from the truth. I had as much support as I wanted—but somehow I chose not to write about it. Instead, the journal was centered on me and my thoughts.

Rings. I had continued to wear Randy's wedding ring, my wedding ring, and my engagement ring on my left hand until eleven months after Randy's death. It was a major decision for me to stop wearing all three rings. However, this event doesn't appear in my memoir; I don't know why I recorded nothing about my decision to remove them. I don't even know how I made that decision. Was there a precipitating event? I don't remember. But occasionally, at night, I pretend I have my old life and wear these rings.

During widowhood, physical activity became a mainstay of my life, and it continues to be—being active, walking, hiking, never sitting still. Activity, even though I often have to force myself to do it, helps my attitude. Does it take away my grief or even lessen it? No, but the endorphins produced by the exercise often clarify my thoughts. Yet my walking and hiking are invisible in my memoir.

My visits to the cemetery continue. In the spring and summer I place fresh flowers at Randy's gravesite, and during the cold months of the year, artificial ones or a wreath. It is my way to honor Randy. This activity may not seem meaningful to others, but I am comforted by and comfortable with my routine. I'm reminded of a story in one of the many grief books I read. A twenty-year-old woman died unexpectedly. The mother of the girl watched the DVD of the memorial service regularly but never went to the cemetery. The father did exactly the opposite—visiting the cemetery frequently, but never watching the DVD. I have the DVD of Randy's service along with the DVD of the pictures that were shown there, but I have never watched either of them. The pain still seems too great. We each have to find our own way through grief and determine what gives us comfort.

Loneliness continues as an unwanted guest. It is difficult to explain to others that half of you is now gone. Part of the loneliness is the absence of touch—the casual touch of your husband, a peck on the cheek, cuddling in bed, holding hands. Things that you took for granted for years are now gone.

It is a couples' world. And although you were aware of it before, it becomes clearer when you are widowed. It's painful to do things by yourself, particularly at first, but you do so. This is what your world will be like, and to move forward you need to take painful steps. The realization that you are no longer part of a couple is hurtful, painful, unwanted.

Throughout the first few months or years, you may seem to take one step forward and then two backward, and so it continues. You have good days and bad days. You have days you want to be with others and days you need solitude. You plan a trip or want to attend an event, but you back out at the last minute. You are on the slippery slope of grief. One day you're doing well, but the next, grief consumes you. This roller coaster becomes your new normal, whether you want it to be or not. But eventually, you see progress in your life. You don't realize it at first, but you are moving forward. It may be in baby steps, but you're moving. And you wonder, how did this happen?

You're not thinking of your husband every minute of the day, but you don't remember when that began to be true. You have no insight into how you're moving forward; the reasons are unclear, unexplainable, and nothing makes sense. And many of us, including me, want to make sense of our lives. But grief has its own rules and making sense is not among them.

Perhaps the title of this memoir, *Finding a Way through Cancer, Dying, and Widowhood*, is misleading. The title makes it sound like I have found my way, that I have the answers, that I'm strong and confident and have worked through my grief. Nothing could be further from the truth. Grief is unpredictable. You won't find a magic recipe, magic words, or answers about how to move forward, only questions. Just as grief is unique to each of us, so is finding our way through it. I have little advice, but I have learned these few things that I pass on to you, and I wish you well.

Give yourself space. Allow the tears to flow when needed, and never be ashamed of your grief or think, "I should be over this." Good days and bad days will continue for some time—and somehow, some way, we need to accept that and move on. Grief doesn't have a timetable, or perhaps it doesn't have *our* timetable.

May you have the strength to find your way through grief. I'm still finding mine.

Bibliography

Edelman, Hope. *Motherless Daughters: The Legacy of Loss.* New York: Delta Trade Paperbacks, 1994.

Sontag, Susan. *Illness as Metaphor.* New York: Farrar, Straus and Giroux, 1988.

Sontag, Susan. *Illness as Metaphor and AIDS and Its Metaphors.* New York: Picador, 1991.

Wagner, Shelly. "Your Questions." In *The Andrew Poems.* Lubbock, TX: Texas Tech University Press, 1994.